500

FRANK LLOYD WRIGHT
REVEALED

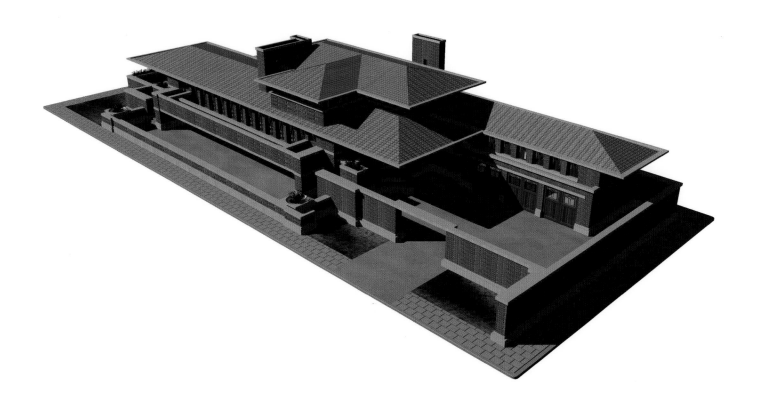

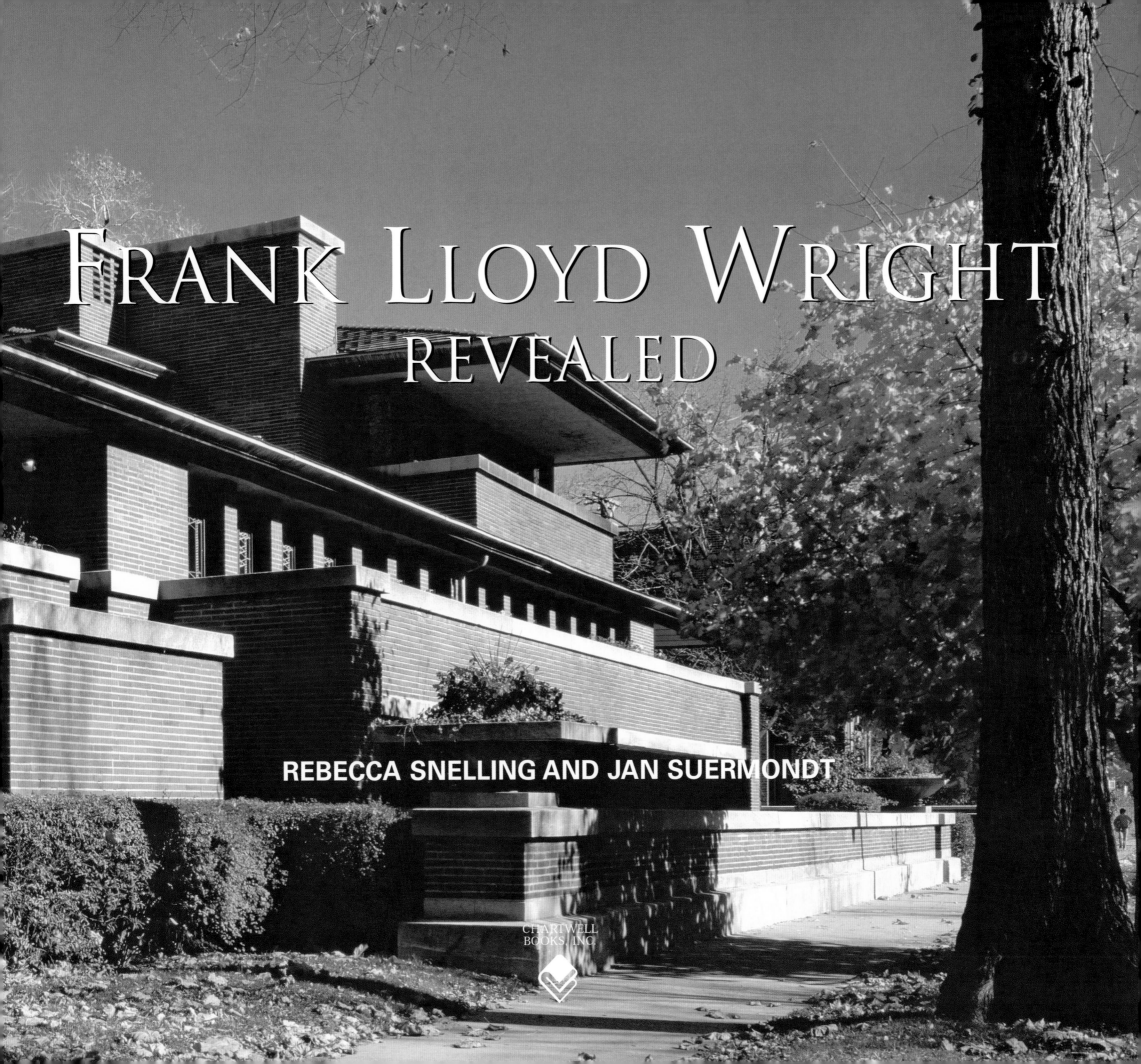

FRANK LLOYD WRIGHT
REVEALED

REBECCA SNELLING AND JAN SUERMONDT

CHARTWELL
BOOKS, INC.

This edition published by:

CHARTWELL BOOKS, INC.
A Division of
BOOK SALES, INC.
114 Northfield Avenue
Edison, New Jersey 08837

ISBN-13: 978-0-7858-2079-6
ISBN-10: 0-7858-2079-5

© 2007 by Compendium Publishing Ltd.,
43 Frith Street, London W1D 4SA,
United Kingdom

Cataloging-in-Publication data is available from
the Library of Congress

Designer: Dave Ball

Color reproduction: anorax

Printed in: China

PAGE 1: *Computer-generated image of the Robie House—one of the finest examples of Wright's Prairie Houses.*

PAGES 2/3: *The real thing—the Robie House stands on the corner between Fifty-ninth Street and Woodlawn, Chicago, Illinois.*

RIGHT: *Fallingwater—Wright's greatest private work.*

FAR RIGHT: *Built from textile blocks in California, the Ennis House has strong Mayan influences.*

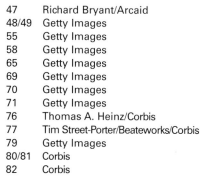

2/3	Richard Bryant/Arcaid	22	Thomas A. Heinz/Corbis	47	Richard Bryant/Arcaid	84	Richard Bryant/Arcaid	136	Alan Weintraub/Arcaid
4	Martin Jones/Arcaid	29	Alan Weintraub/Arcaid	48/49	Getty Images	90/91	Catherine Karnow/Corbis	140	Alan Weintraub/Arcaid
5	Getty Images	30	Richard Bryant/Arcaid	55	Getty Images	92	Getty Images	141	Alan Weintraub/Arcaid
6/7	Natalie Tepper/Arcaid	34	Richard Bryant/Arcaid	58	Getty Images	93	Getty Images	142	Alan Weintraub/Arcaid
8	Leonard de Selva/Corbis	35	Alan Weintraub/Arcaid	65	Getty Images	95	Richard Bryant/Arcaid	146	Alan Weintraub/Arcaid
8	Time Life Pictures/Getty Images	36	Farrell Grehan/Corbis	69	Getty Images	107	Martin Jones/Arcaid	148	Alan Weintraub/Arcaid
9	Thomas A. Heinz/Corbis	36	Richard Bryant/Arcaid	70	Getty Images	108/109	Richard Bryant/Arcaid	150	Alan Weintraub/Arcaid
10/11	Angelo Hornak/Corbis	38	Alan Weintraub/Arcaid	71	Getty Images	111	Natalie Tepper/Arcaid	151	Alan Weintraub/Arcaid
12	Getty Images	39	Alan Weintraub/Arcaid	76	Thomas A. Heinz/Corbis	112	Thomas A. Heinz/Arcaid	152	Alan Weintraub/Arcaid
13	Farrell Grehan/Corbis	40	Alan Weintraub/Arcaid	77	Tim Street-Porter/Beateworks/Corbis	120	Thomas A. Heinz/Arcaid	153	Alan Weintraub/Arcaid
14/15	Richard Bryant/Arcaid	41	Alan Weintraub/Arcaid	79	Getty Images	125	Thomas A. Heinz/Arcaid	156	Alan Weintraub/Arcaid
16	Richard Bryant/Arcaid	44		80/81	Corbis	128	Alan Weintraub/Arcaid	157	Alan Weintraub/Arcaid
18	Alan Weintraub/Arcaid	44	Farrell Grehan/Corbis	82	Corbis	131	Alan Weintraub/Arcaid		

CONTENTS

Introduction

INTRODUCTION

ABOVE: *April 1946: Architect Frank Lloyd Wright surrounded by students at his home.*

RIGHT: *Fallingwater—as drawn by Walter DuBois Richards—was one of 16 stamps honoring great American architecture. On February 4, 1998, the Robie House also appeared on a U.S.postage stamp.*

FAR RIGHT: *Art-glass dining room ceiling light from the Ward Willits House designed by the Studio of Frank Lloyd Wright.*

Frank Lloyd Wright 1867-1959 Fallingwater Mill Run PA
Architecture USA 20c

Frank Lloyd Wright, born in 1867 in Wisconsin, was one of the most prolific and influential architects of the twentieth century. Throughout his long life he drew up designs for more than eleven hundred buildings, which included houses, churches, schools, libraries, offices, and museums. Of those plans, more than four hundred were built, with more than twenty now open to the public. He also designed furniture, soft furnishings, tableware, lamps, birdhouses, dog kennels, plus much more, and he was a respected author, lecturer, philosopher, and social commentator.

Although Wright gained a high profile through iconic buildings such as the Guggenheim Museum in New York, it was housing that preoccupied him throughout his career and his importance as an architect is often said to be his evolution of the affordable family house.

In the late nineteenth century, when Wright began working in Chicago, huge social and economic changes were under way in America and it was his awareness of and reaction to these shifts that marked him out from contemporary architects. At this time American domestic architecture had no clear voice of its own. Styles were a mishmash of borrowed European influences, built out of context and with no regard to the emerging American way of life. Wright changed this and developed an architectural language that was unique to

the country and yet came to have a worldwide influence: aspects of his designs can be found in a large proportion of houses built today and the familiar American ranch house is directly attributable to Wright's Prairie houses.

INFLUENCES AND BELIEFS

Wright's architectural concepts were rooted in his upbringing. Sent to labor on farms during his school summer vacations, he acquired a lifelong passion for nature and the natural environment that was to underpin all his work. There he observed natural landforms, the patterns of trees, shapes in the landscape, the flow of water. From his father he gained knowledge of music and its structure, and his mother bought him Froebel blocks (geometrically shaped blocks that could be assembled to form three-dimensional structures) to play with-an influence evident in the geometric basis of his buildings.

Wright was also widely read and interested in literature, poetry, and philosophy: He believed in instinct, and intellectual and spiritual individualism. Yet at the same time he was a student of civil engineering, with a firm grasp of structure and technology and a willingness to embrace the emerging technology and materials of the industrial revolution.

From this background Wright formed his abiding principles of "organic" architecture. By this he meant that

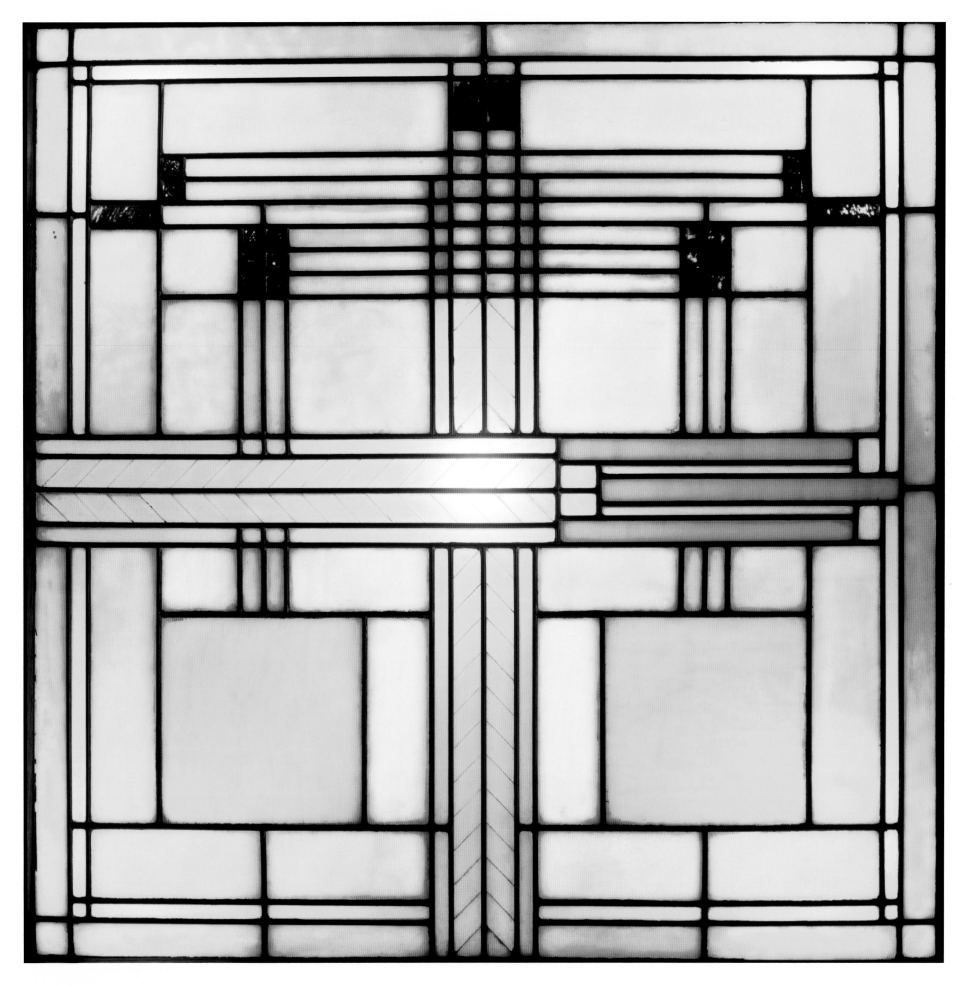

buildings should fit into their environment and be a product of their place, purpose, and time-they should interpret the principles of nature. The term also meant a harmonious relationship between the form (design) of a building and its function, and the honest use of materials, allowing their inherent properties to shine with no pretence at disguise (he never painted wood, for example). His philosophy-in line with the Arts and Crafts movement that flourished in Britain, Europe, and America from the 1880s to World War I-extended to every detail of the house: Furniture, carpets, doors, lighting, and ornamental pieces were all designed to integrate and please the eye, to create unity.

Driving these ideas was Wright's desire to create a space where the human soul could be nourished and flourish. Human values were paramount. He believed that an attractive living environment enhanced the well being of society and he believed passionately that people should live close to the outdoors, be near nature. It was also his view that compartmentalizing houses was detrimental to family life and he wanted to give interior space a new freedom.

THE PRAIRIE STYLE

These concepts manifested themselves from about 1900 to 1920 in what came to be known as the Prairie Style-designs suited to the flat Midwest. The houses were horizontal rather than vertical in outline, sitting low on the prairie lands. They were seldom more than two stories, often with single-story wings or extensions. Wright did away with little-used basements and placed the house on a defined platform, bonding it to the ground. Mortar courses between the brickwork were deepened and vertical joints colored to match, thus emphasizing horizontal lines. Roof lines were low and oversized,

RIGHT: *The Guggenheim Museum in New York is cleverly designed to fit into a tight and awkwardly shaped site. It is one of Frank Lloyd Wright's greatest masterpieces.*

often extending far beyond the walls, both anchoring and sheltering the houses, keeping them safe and near to the ground. He wanted the occupants to be protected. Chimneys were squat and broad, in keeping with the horizontal outline but not to be ignored: They were a potent symbol of the hearth inside the home, the heart of family life as he saw it.

Cantilever construction was one of Wright's greatest devices. Taking his inspiration from the branches of trees, the wings of birds, and overhanging rock formations, he elevated terraces and balconies, created layers above ground level, opened up interior spaces, and took away the square, supporting corners of the conventional house "block." Plans could be simple or complex, but the essential tenets remained.

USONIAN

Although with the Prairie Style Wright had broken away from the physical constraints of Victorian architecture, to his mind he was still designing "undemocratic" houses, with servants' quarters and utility areas such as kitchens set apart from the main living area, and costs exceeding the budget of most American families. His longstanding dream was to design mass-produced homes for the American middle classes that were functional and aesthetically pleasing, but above all affordable, and in the Depression years of the 1930s this was his main focus. So came his revolutionary Usonian houses (Usonian being a poetic abbreviation of United States of North America). He kept sight of the goals he aimed for in his Prairie houses, but adapted them to a smaller budget.

Wright's "true" Usonian houses-beginning with the first Jacobs Residence in 1936-were small (no more than about fifteen hundred square feet), usually single-story, pared down, energy-efficient, and constructed with modular, standardized components to minimize labor and therefore cost. Gone were the servant's quarters and the dining room; the kitchen,

ABOVE: *Frank Lloyd Wright's buildings were known for their art glass.*

LEFT: *The sitting room at Fallingwater, the iconic vacation house that Frank Lloyd Wright designed for wealthy businessman Edgar J. Kaufmann in 1935.*

now known as the "workspace," became an important and integral part of the open-plan living area and a carport (Wright's invention as a replacement for the more costly garage) reflected the explosion in car ownership that had swept across America.

Wright's commitment to designing affordable, quality homes never wavered and he continued to develop the theme up until his death in 1959, by which time he had designed more than 300 Usonian houses, of which around 140 were built. These included his Usonian Automatics, which came in kit form-so rose "automatically" -and the 1950s Erdman prefabricated houses.

The Frank Lloyd Wright Foundation, established in 1940 by Wright and his third wife, Olgivanna, holds the lifework of Frank Lloyd Wright. Its international headquarters are at Taliesin West in Scottsdale, Arizona.

CHAPTER I
THE ROBIE HOUSE

THE ROBIE HOUSE

HISTORY

The Robie House is another of Wright's best-known works and one of the finest examples of the Prairie School, the style of architecture defined and developed by Wright and some of his contemporaries in Chicago in the first decade of the twentieth century. Like Fallingwater, it has been designated a historic landmark. It stands on the corner between Fifty-ninth Street and Woodlawn, next to the University of Chicago campus, in Chicago, Illinois.

It was built for Frederick C. Robie and his wife, Lora, between 1906 and 1909. Robie was the son of George T. Robie, who founded the Excelsior Company in Chicago, which marketed sewing-machine supplies; in the 1880s he expanded into the bicycle manufacturing business. Frederick studied mechanical engineering at Purdue University, in West Lafayette, Indiana, before entering his father's business in 1899. Shortly after he met Lora Hieronymus at a University of Chicago dance and married her in 1902. By 1906, aged thirty-three, Robie was making substantial sums of money and had plans to build a lavish house. With this in mind he and Lora bought the narrow plot of land on which Robie House stands. (Lora had been a student at the university and was still active on the campus, so wanted to be close by.)

Frederick had his own clear ideas about the sort of house he wanted—

uninterrupted spaces, views, natural light, none of the conventional, unimaginative soft furnishings prevalent at the time-and had sketched out some thoughts for a house before knowing of Wright. As an engineer he wanted the house to function as efficiently as a machine. After showing the drawings to friends and colleagues, he was advised that Wright was the architect most likely to be in tune with his ideals and concepts. This proved to be the case and Robie commissioned Wright promptly after meeting him. Wright designed the house in his Oak Park studio and it was completed for a total cost of $59,000, a sum that included the purchase of the land and all the furnishings, also designed by Wright, and the architect's fee of $8,000. It was to be one of the last commissions for the studio as in 1909 Wright abandoned both his family and his Oak Park practice to elope with Mamah Cheney, whose husband had been one of Wright's clients.

Robie and his family moved into the house in the spring of 1910, but they didn't own it for long: Having spent just one-and-a-half years in the house, Robie had to sell it after his father's death to pay off debts. This also coincided with the failure of his marriage. David Lee Taylor, president of an advertising company, bought the house but he died ten months later. His widow sold it to Marshall Dodge Wilber, treasurer of the Wilber Mercantile Agency and commodore

RIGHT: *The Robie House became the template for future Prairie-style homes—the horizontal themes were composed of low-pitched hipped roofs with wide overhanging eaves and cantilevered ends, plus long running bands of windows letting in as much light as possible. All this was achieved with a minimum of decoration and embellishment to give a clean and modern silhouette to the building.*

of the Chicago Yacht Club. The Wilbers were lavish hosts-inviting up to two hundred guests at any one time to lunch at the house. According to Mrs. Wilber's diary, Wright came back three times while they lived in the house to look it over. He told her that "this is the best example of my work" and that he wanted to buy it himself and live there one day. It was not to be.

The house remained in the Wilbers' ownership until 1926 when they sold it, along with all its furnishings, to the Chicago Theological Seminary, which had moved in on the other side of the street. This marked the beginning of decades of misuse and neglect for the house, from which it nearly didn't recover. The seminary used it as a dormitory for married students for many years and then in 1941 announced the school needed more accommodation space and that it planned to demolish the house so that a new dormitory could be built. Public pressure against this, however-which included correspondence from Wright-caused the plans to be dropped.

In 1957 the specter of demolition rose again and this time, due to the clamor of conservationists, local protestors, and the press, the Commission on Chicago Landmarks was founded, with the Robie House becoming the first building to be designated a Chicago landmark. Wright himself, by then ninety, had added his weight to the appeal by visiting the house, recalling, with customary lack of modesty, that it was as beautiful as it had been when he designed it a half-century earlier.

Later that year Webb and Knapp, the New York real estate development firm in charge of much of the urban renewal in the surrounding Hyde Park neighborhood, purchased the house for $125,000. Rumor had it that Wright had persuaded William Zeckendorf, head of the firm, to come to the rescue. The firm used it as their construction offices until 1963, when they donated the house to the University of Chicago, which owns it to this day. During a formal ceremony the Robie House deed

RIGHT: *Experts consider the Robie House was a turning point in modern domestic architecture. As such, it has been voted in the top ten most important buildings in the United States.*

LEFT: *Wright preferred to use Roman bricks for his Prairie houses. This is a size rarely made today (and proved hugely problematic when the Robie House was being restored). It is 4 x 2 x 12in, which is longer and narrower than standard bricks. The effect is to visually enhance the horizontal theme of the building.*

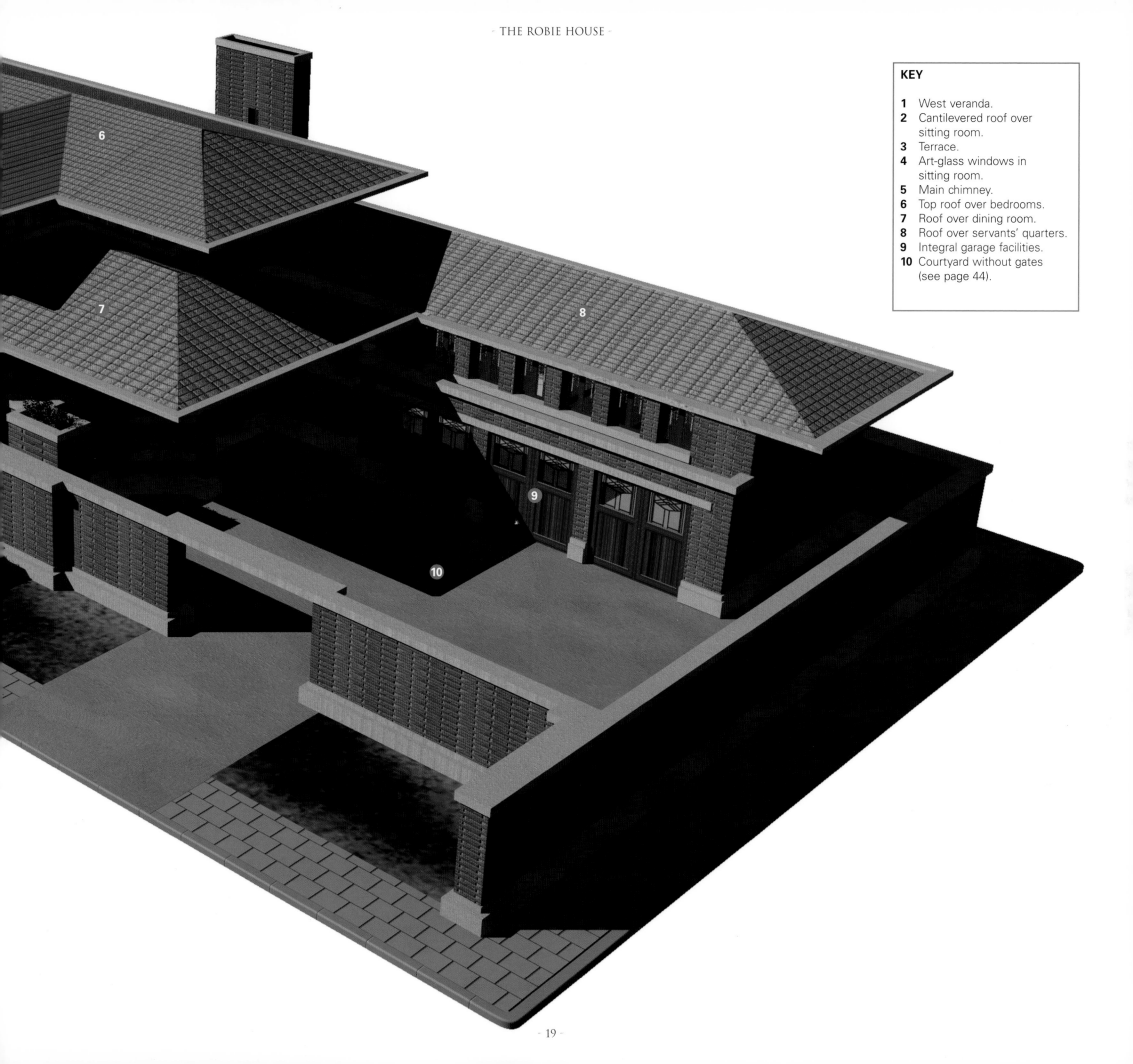

KEY

1 West veranda.
2 Cantilevered roof over sitting room.
3 Terrace.
4 Art-glass windows in sitting room.
5 Main chimney.
6 Top roof over bedrooms.
7 Roof over dining room.
8 Roof over servants' quarters.
9 Integral garage facilities.
10 Courtyard without gates (see page 44).

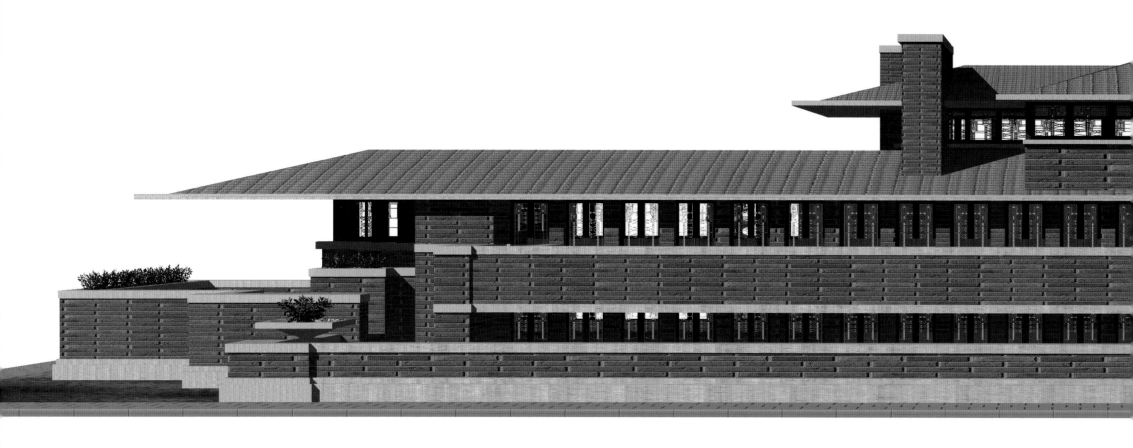

ABOVE: *Front elevation. Wright designed the Robie House in 1908 while he was still working from his Oak Park Studio. Completed by 1910 the building was totally innovative, its strong horizontal lines with the use of cantilevers and wide open-plan interior spaces won it the sobriquet "Prairie House Style." The overhanging eaves are precisely designed so that the blistering midsummer sun hardly reaches the base of the south-facing living room windows.*

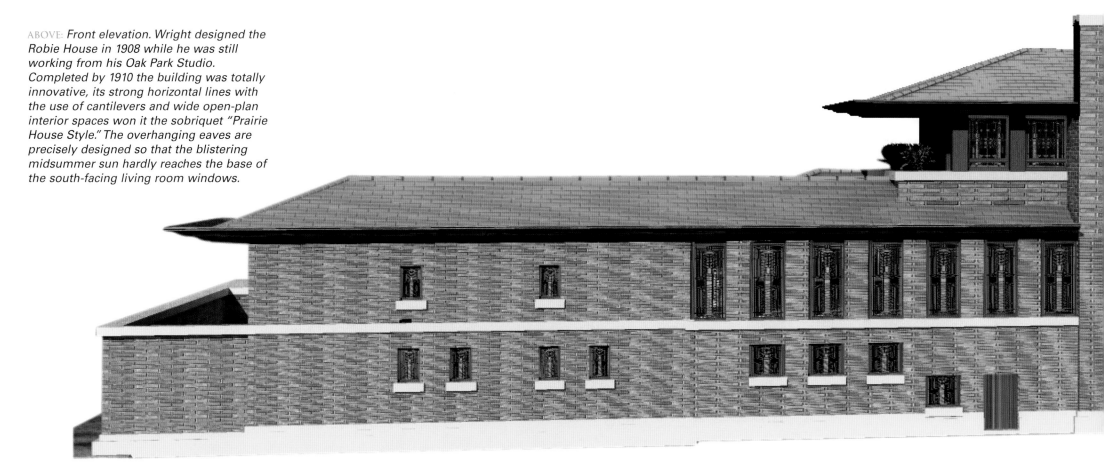

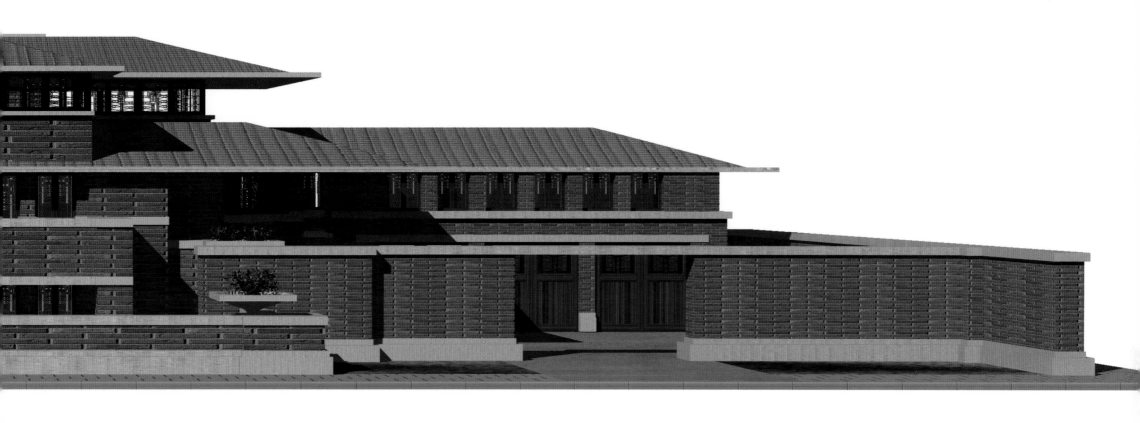

BELOW: *Rear elevation with west veranda to the right. The entrance to the house is on this side, just before the steps to the veranda. Frank Lloyd Wright was inspired by the open prairie grasslands and wide open horizons of his native American Midwest for the design.*

LEFT: *The principal living room. The rooms are in the process of being restored to their former glory. This is a costly and meticulous process that will take a number of years to complete.*

BELOW: *The interior is open plan—a great innovation at a time when households were compartmentalized into different specified areas. The heart of the house was the central fireplace from where the spaces radiate out.*

was handed over to the university's incumbent president, George W. Beadle. In the same year the house was registered as a National Historic Landmark. For more than thirty years the university used the house, first as the Adlai Stevenson Institute for International Peace and then as offices of the Alumni Association.

During this time the building was showing some of the problems commonly associated with Wright's work-instability of the cantilevered structures and damp damage from the leaking roofs. Well-intentioned but clumsy attempts at shoring up and repointing the brickwork only contributed further to its by now parlous state. Robie House nevertheless became a place of pilgrimage for architecture buffs and hopes that it would eventually be restored were realized in 1997 when the Frank Lloyd Preservation Trust stepped in. They signed a lease at a ceremony at the house on January 24, pledging to open the

house to the public as an architectural museum and restore the now very badly deteriorated fabric of the building and its original contents to pristine condition. Wright's masterpiece was safe.

THE HOUSE DESCRIBED

Of the seventy-five or so buildings Wright built in the Chicago area, none has become as well known as the Robie House. When it was first constructed, it was referred to locally as "The Battleship," and with its streamlined, long, low silhouette, sharp lines, and continuous limestone sills resembling railings, it is easy to see why. Standing on its narrow plot in a leafy, urban street, the Robie House is dramatically unlike any of its neighbors, even though most were built little more than ten years previously.

The house, as an exemplary and sophisticated example of the Prairie Style, has all the expected features: exaggerated

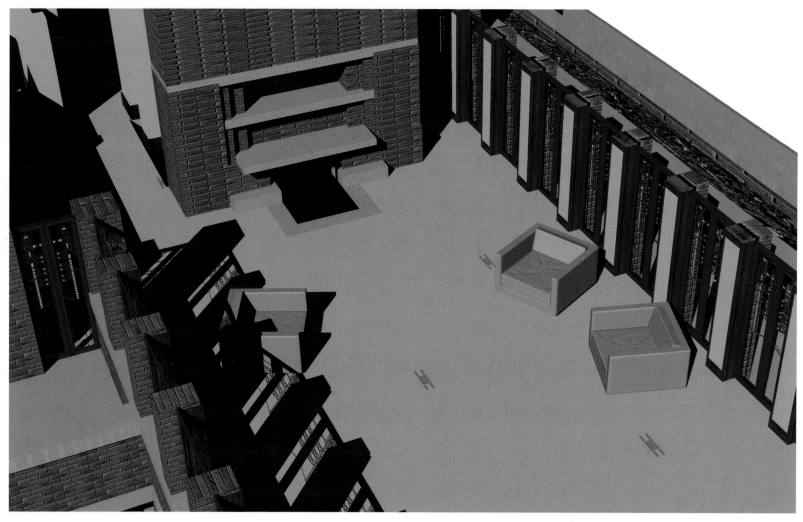

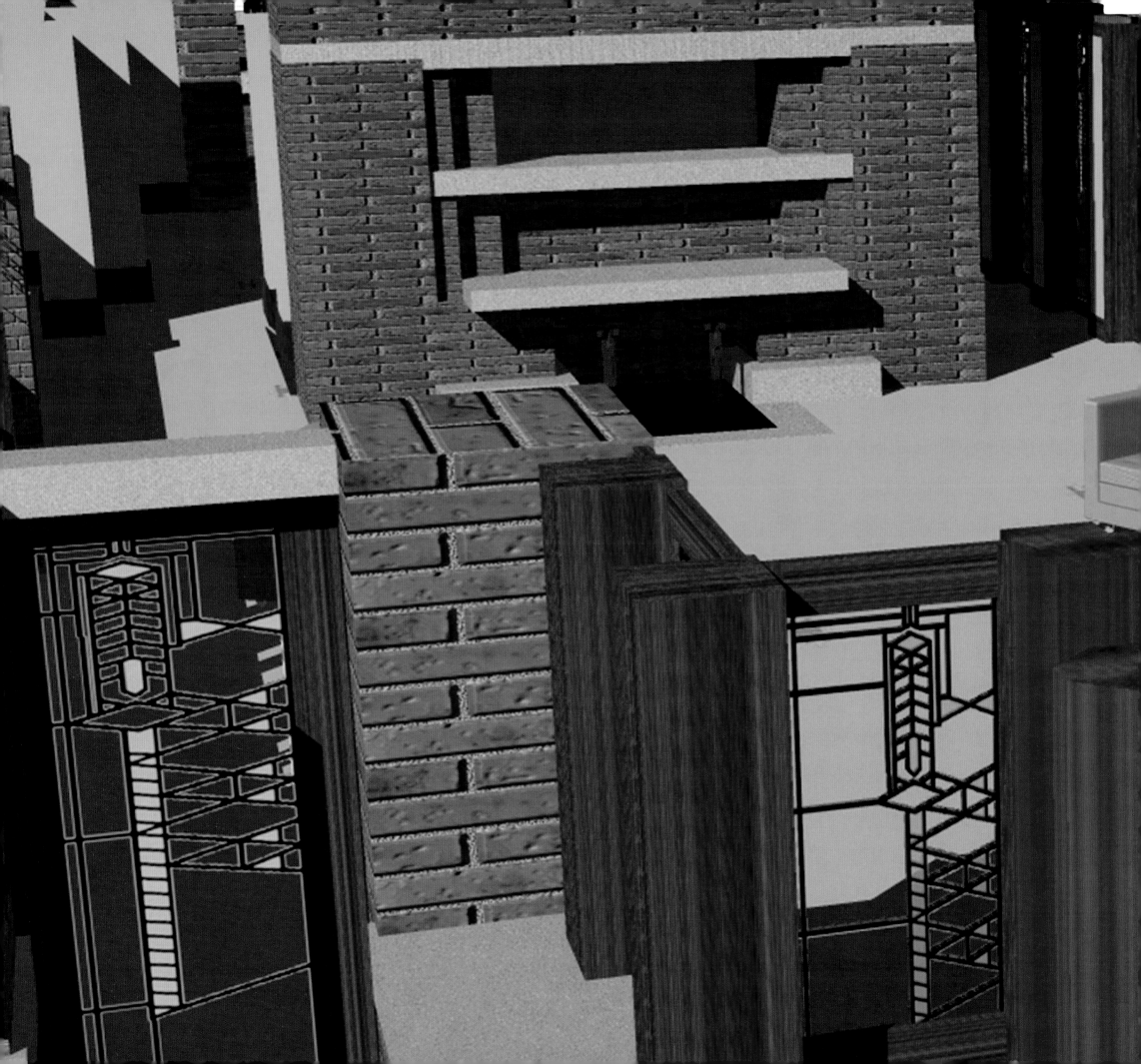

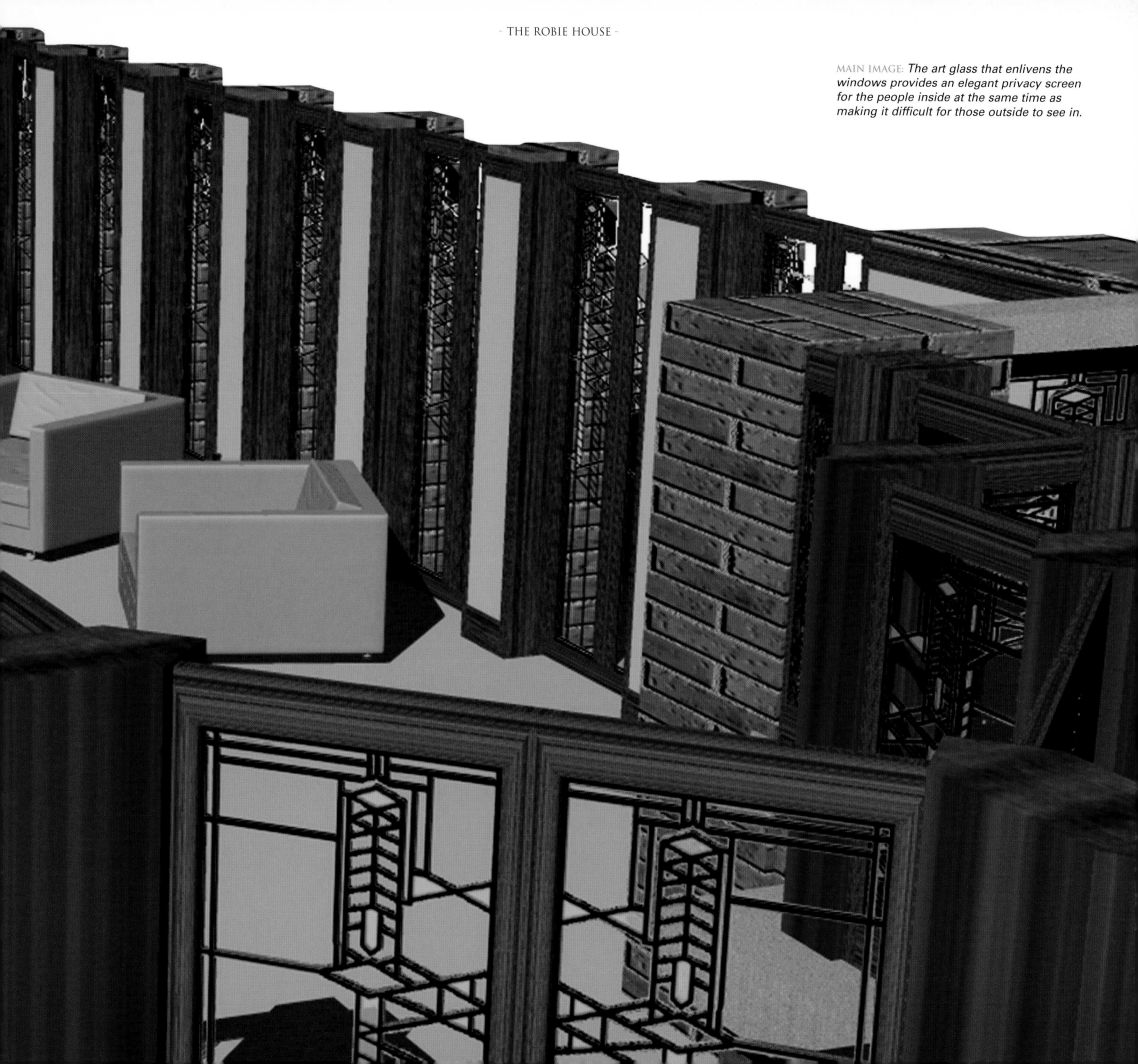

MAIN IMAGE: *The art glass that enlivens the windows provides an elegant privacy screen for the people inside at the same time as making it difficult for those outside to see in.*

overhangs on low-pitched roofs, giving the appearance that they are floating; pillars; smooth lines; interlocking levels; horizontal bands of parapets and cantilevered balconies; recessed bands of casement windows; shadowy spaces; a large, square chimney stack; open porches; lack of fiddly ornamentation; the predominate use of stone, concrete, metal, and glass, with unpainted wood trim inside. The low-lying effect is enhanced by the parallel layers of brickwork (the bricks are exceptionally long and narrow, with the cement raked out for emphasis on the horizontals and the uprights filled in with brick-colored mortar so they disappear) alternating with the pale yellow limestone of the base plinth and copings to the balconies and terraces.

To compensate for the lack of a yard, Wright built into the terraces and balconies lots of large, angular, copper-lined planters, window boxes and square urns to visually soften the edges of the building and to maintain the relationship with nature he considered so important. At each level there is a terrace, balcony, or porch to allow the residents ready access to the open air. A low retaining wall encloses the slimmest of front yards.

There are three stories to the house, but they are not clearly evident and the overall impression is that there is one main floor with a small addition above. In fact the overall height is no more than most two-story houses of the same era. The plan of the building consists of a pair of long, two-story sections, each only a room deep, which lie parallel with each other but are staggered so that they abut along about half their length. The main block, which faces the street at the front of the house, contains the principal living spaces, while the narrower block behind contains rooms that require privacy or are purely utilitarian. Two diamond-shaped bays at each end of the font block, overhung by the extended

RIGHT: *A strong theme of the house is the use of glass and light. This is seen to best effect on the main level where the entire south wall consists of paired art-glass French doors, which open out onto a long balcony.*

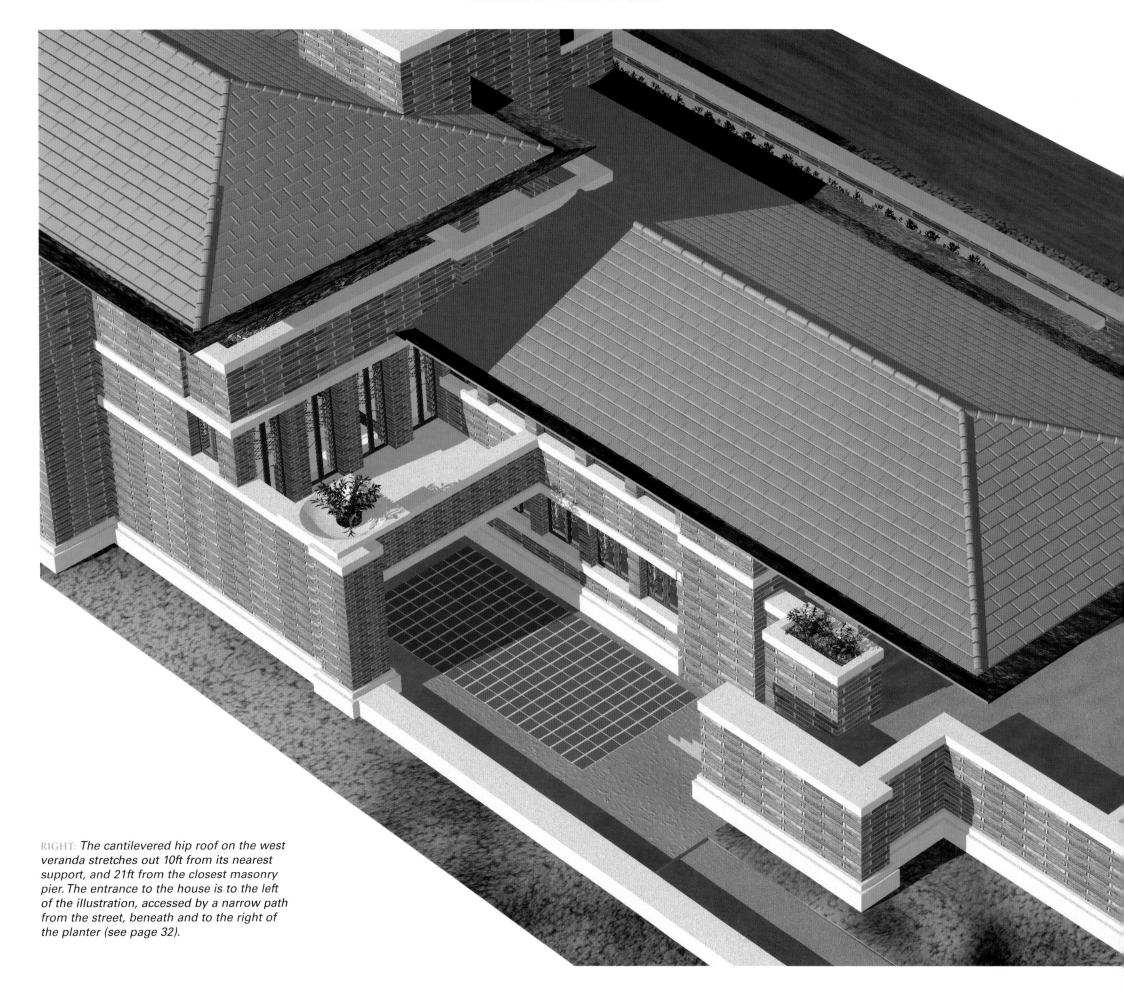

RIGHT: *The cantilevered hip roof on the west veranda stretches out 10ft from its nearest support, and 21ft from the closest masonry pier. The entrance to the house is to the left of the illustration, accessed by a narrow path from the street, beneath and to the right of the planter (see page 32).*

RIGHT: *Almost the only ornamentation allowed in the Robie House are some stunning art-glass pieces that were specifically designed for the project by Wright himself. He viewed these as "light screens" and used them as a passageway between the outside space and the interior. In his words, "Now the outside may come inside, and the inside may, and does, go outside."*

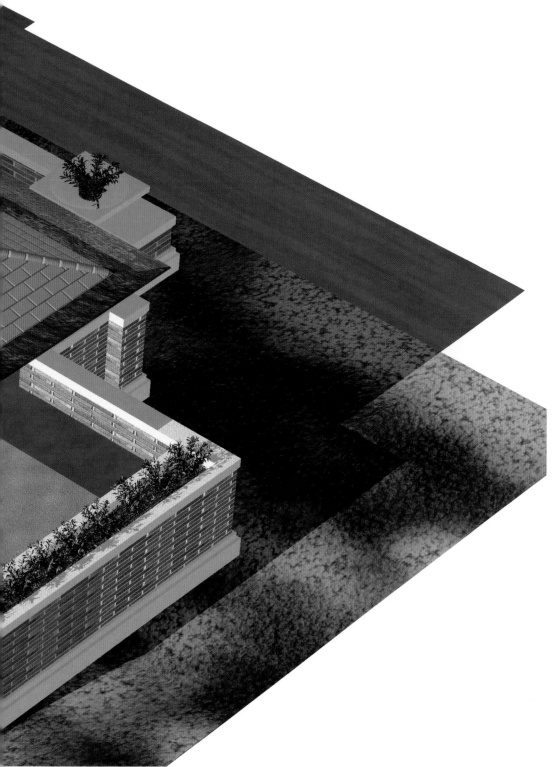

roof canopy to provide protection from sun and rain, have been likened to the bows of a ship. On top is the much smaller, square third story: the great vessel's "chimney."

There is no welcoming front to the house, and with the effect of presenting an impenetrable, private face to the street, the entrance to the house is on the north side, at the eastern end of the rear block. This is a far cry from the facades of neighboring houses. Low and without any attempt at grandeur, the door leads into a small, rather dark reception hall. Occupying the lower level of the main, street-facing block are the children's playroom and the billiard room. Behind the playroom, in the parallel block, is the utility room and laundry room, with what was originally the garage (now a shop) extending in the same line beyond

the front block. In front of the garage is the courtyard, screened from the street by a high brick wall. Robie was a great lover of automobiles (his business later diversified into automobile parts) and not only was this house one of the first in America to have an integral garage-and housing more than one car at that-the garage also had an engine pit and a car wash built in to it. (The original design of the garage was altered some years after it was built.)

From the entrance hall a short, steep, narrow staircase leads through an arch in the central chimney block up to the first floor of the front main block. Emerging into the first floor space from the small landing at the top of the stairs is like entering a different world. Wright was very aware of the power of contrast and surprise, and by

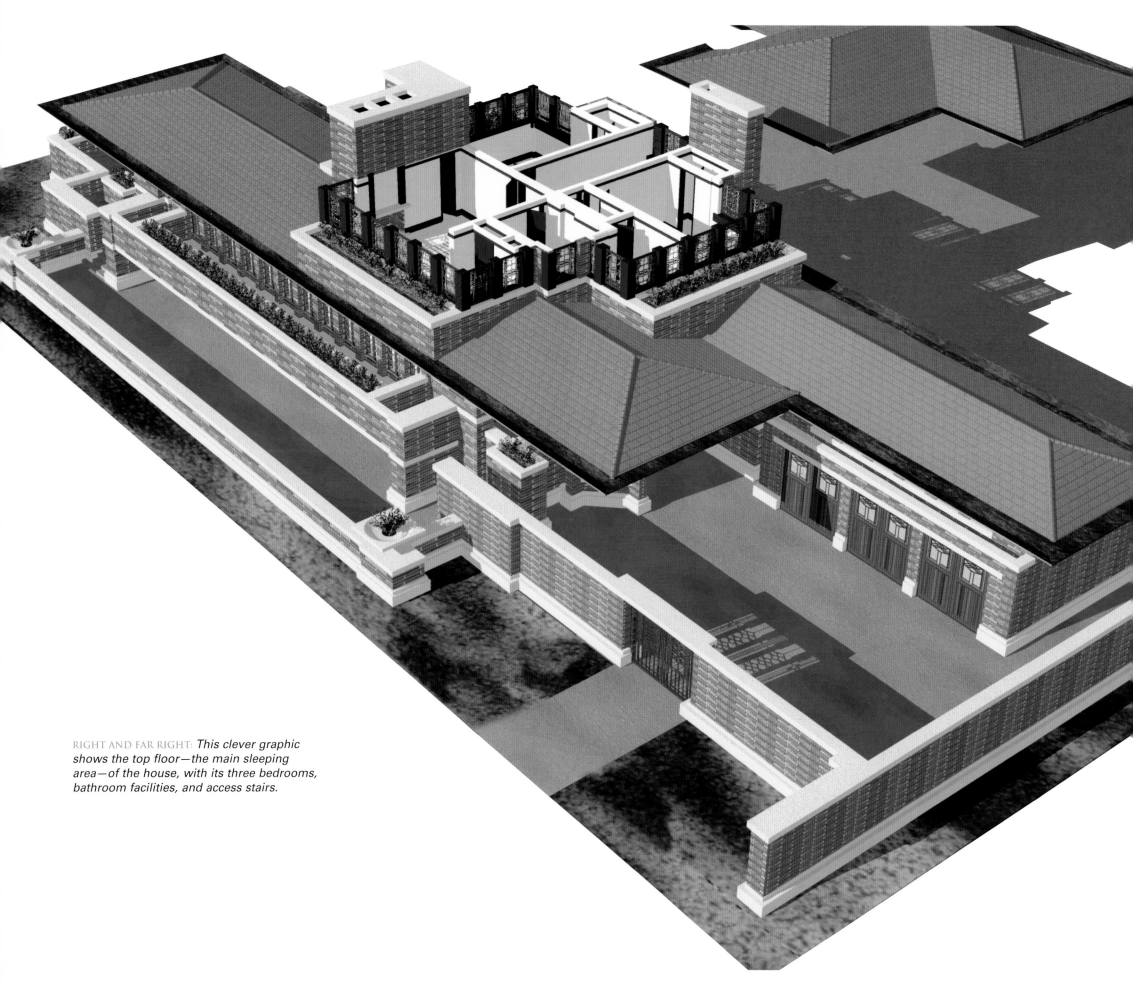

RIGHT AND FAR RIGHT: *This clever graphic shows the top floor—the main sleeping area—of the house, with its three bedrooms, bathroom facilities, and access stairs.*

prolonging and disguising the entry into the pièce de résistance of the house he heightened the visitor's delight and surprise on arrival.

This is the main living area of the house, the free-flowing space Wright espoused, acknowledging a less formal way of life and encouraging family activities and interaction. There seem to be no real walls to the room. The so-called living and dining rooms are separated only by a large H-shaped fireplace in the middle of the room: the heart of family life. Two wide brick columns support the broad brick chimney

breast, which is cut away to reduce the barrier effect and provide a visual link to both sides of the space. The fire pit is sunk into the floor within a plain concrete hearth, with a concrete mantelpiece above.

The three outside walls of the huge room consist almost entirely of glass, broken up by narrow plaster-faced pillars neatly edged all round with square-cut oak trim. Everything aligns. Several pairs of glass doors extending from floor to ceiling open along the length of the south-facing balcony and the bands of windows are set at waist height. At either end of the rooms

the diagonal bay windows lead out to the terraces. The leaded glass (or art glass) windows in the house are one of its particularly striking features and in this room are stunning. They are made of clear plate glass and colored cathedral glass, with copper-plated zinc joints (cames) holding the panes in place. Designs are geometric, often featuring triangles and flattened diamond shapes, echoing the diamond bays at the ends of the room. They are delicate enough not to block out too much sunlight, yet provide just enough privacy for the residents. The casements

that Wright insisted upon provided the ideal canvas for his designs in a way that sash windows could not.

The ceiling height steps up from the perimeter of the room, going from about eight feet to ten. (Wright was about 5 feet 8 inches tall, and although it has been said that this contributed to the relatively low ceiling heights characteristic of his buildings, it is just as likely that they concurred with his ideas of democracy and his conviction that houses should make the occupants feel sheltered and protected.) In fact the step is a device to conceal the two

ABOVE: *Frederick C. Robie was a prosperous Chicago bicycle manufacturer until his business fell on hard times and he went bankrupt. In 1926 his beautiful, innovative house became a dormitory for the Chicago Theological Seminary. In the 1950s the Robie House became a landmark building again, this time as the first building to be preserved for its architectural importance and was the recipient of Chicago's first landmark protection ordinance.*

MAIN IMAGE: *West veranda showing entrance. It is difficult to appreciate in the graphic and (as above) in real life the subtleties Wright employed to construct a three-story building without increasing height.*

steel beams that support the roof cantilevers. Flat strips of polished wood of different widths, precisely spaced to align with the doorposts, follow the step and run in neat rectilinear lines across the ceiling.

Electric lighting comes from high rows of glass globes held in square wooden frames of wood and suspended by open, sculpted blocks, and the laylights, screened with glass and decorative blocks, that create a consistent light around the edge of the room. Elsewhere in the house exquisitely designed square, bronze fixtures were fitted with half-sphere glass coverings and placed with careful attention to their falling shadow.

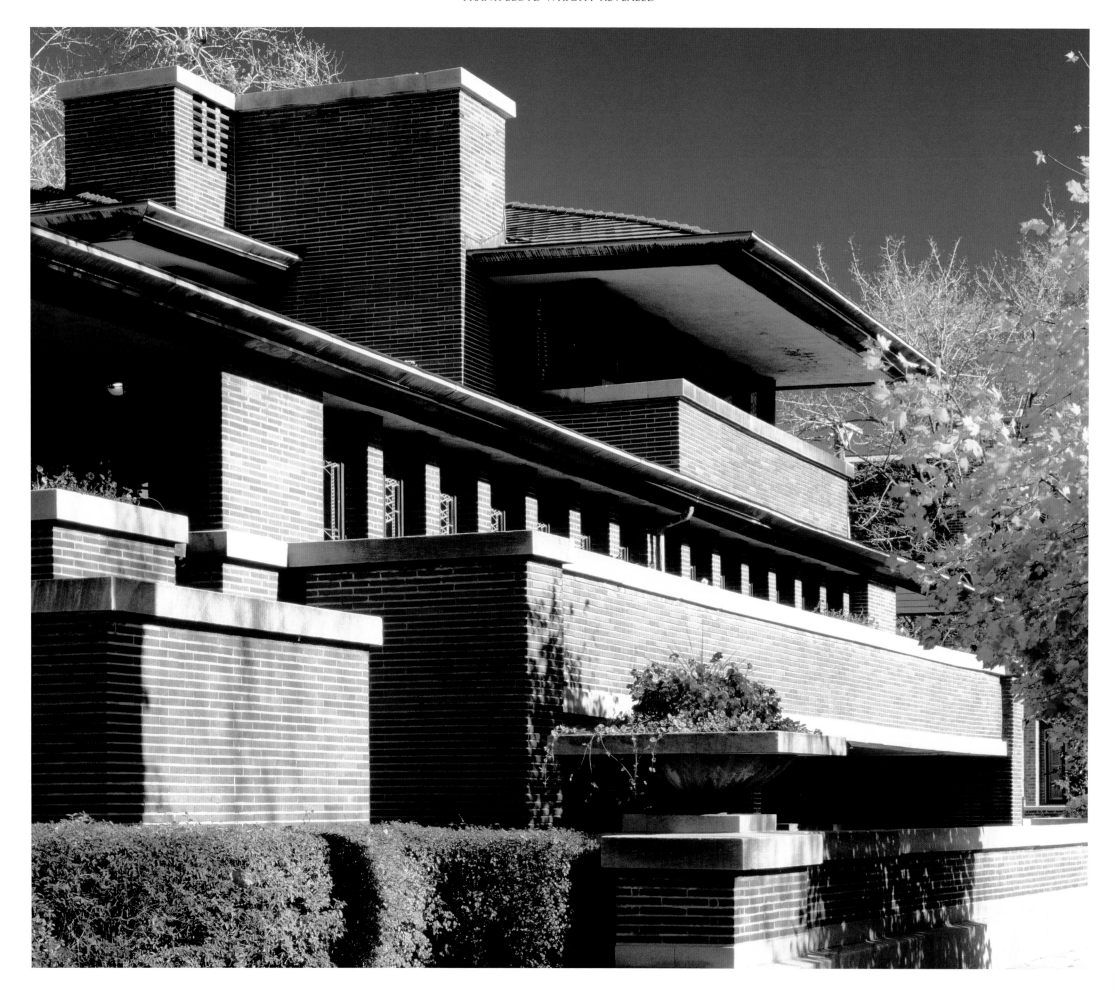

LEFT: *Extensive restoration was completed in 2003 with the exterior at last structurally stable. The conservators then turned their attention to the long term project of restoring the much neglected interior.*

ABOVE: *The living room and dining room contain huge laylights in their ceilings. These are wooden grilles with decorative blocks and sandblasted glass that screen the incandescent lights to produce a warm glow around the edges of the rooms.*

RIGHT: *The house contains 174 art-glass windows made up of clear "cathedral" plate glass broken up by geometric, copper plated zinc leading holding small, predominantly triangular, pieces of colored glass. The designs are mostly abstract representations of flowers and plants.*

FAR RIGHT: *The long gallery of art-glass French windows divide the principal room from the veranda.*

The rectangular six-seater dining table is a powerful feature of the room in its own right and one of Wright's most famous pieces of furniture. There are four square posts at the corners large enough to hold glass lamps, candles, and flowers. Practical as always and in line with his passion for uncluttered spaces, Wright conceived the design to take such decorations off the table and so eliminate all visual and symbolic barriers between the diners. The chairs, with their exceptionally high slatted backs that continue right to the ground, not only provide a backdrop to the face of the person seated, but further contribute to the sense of intimacy around the table: almost creating a room within a room.

The floor covering features a single geometric motif that echoes the shapes elsewhere in the room. All the colors—soft browns and ochers—harmonize.

Other pieces of furniture designed by Wright especially for the house are small, square, wooden stools that could double as chairside tables and low wooden coffee tables—some with glass tops. A low upholstered sofa has wooden extensions to the arms, creating side tables. Radiator grills below the windows on the north side of the room are made in matching slatted wood. In front of the doors, the heating is set into the floor beneath brass grilles. At the back of the living room block, in the parallel, staggered block, is a guest room, the kitchen, and three small rooms used as servants' quarters, all laid end to end.

The bedrooms are up on the third floor, clustered around the central chimney mass, where the two lower blocks overlap, forming a sort of truncated tower. Typically

ABOVE: Wright considered the furnishings to be integral to the building and—in the Robie House as elsewhere in other projects—incorporated a number of built-in seats and structures as part of the design. He also liked to design as much of the furniture as the client would permit.

ABOVE: *The only distinction between the living and dining space is the central fireplace chimney. All the latest modern amenities (electrical systems etc) were designed into the fabric of the building so as* *not to intrude on the visual effect. This concept was a completely radical idea that took American society by storm and became a popular demand for new buildings across the land.*

LEFT: *The Robie House was rescued for $125,000 by New York architectural firm Webb and Knapp. They used the house as their construction office during their Urban Renewal work in Hyde Park, then in 1963 gave the building to the University of Chicago.*

BELOW: *The lights and fittings were especially designed for the house. In particular these wonderful sconces that adorn the rooms are sculptural works of art in their own right. Unfortunately many have been removed and those remaining are in desperate need of conservation.*

they are not particularly large rooms, but cozy, private retreats providing contrast to the open, public space below. The master bedroom has its own bathroom and a fireplace and there is a terrace.

TODAY

Since the Frank Lloyd Preservation Trust took over the care of the house in 1997, extensive repair and restoration work has been carried out as part of a ten-year, $8 million project. Funds have included a $250,000 federal Save America's Treasures (SAT) grant and $1 million in private SAT funds. The Frank Lloyd Wright Preservation Trust has raised the remaining funds.

The house's checkered history and various uses had taken a severe toll both inside and out. Initially considerable research and analysis had to be undertaken, involving examination of historical records and consultation with knowledgeable followers of Wright and specialist restoration architects. Painstakingly detailed documentation of the house and its components as it stood was also necessary before work could begin. Because the house was going to be

MAIN IMAGE: *Roof off. The Robie House was a conscious revolt by Wright against the currently prevailing historical revival style and an—as it turned out—enormously successful attempt to devise an indigenous American architectural style that combined functionality with beauty.*

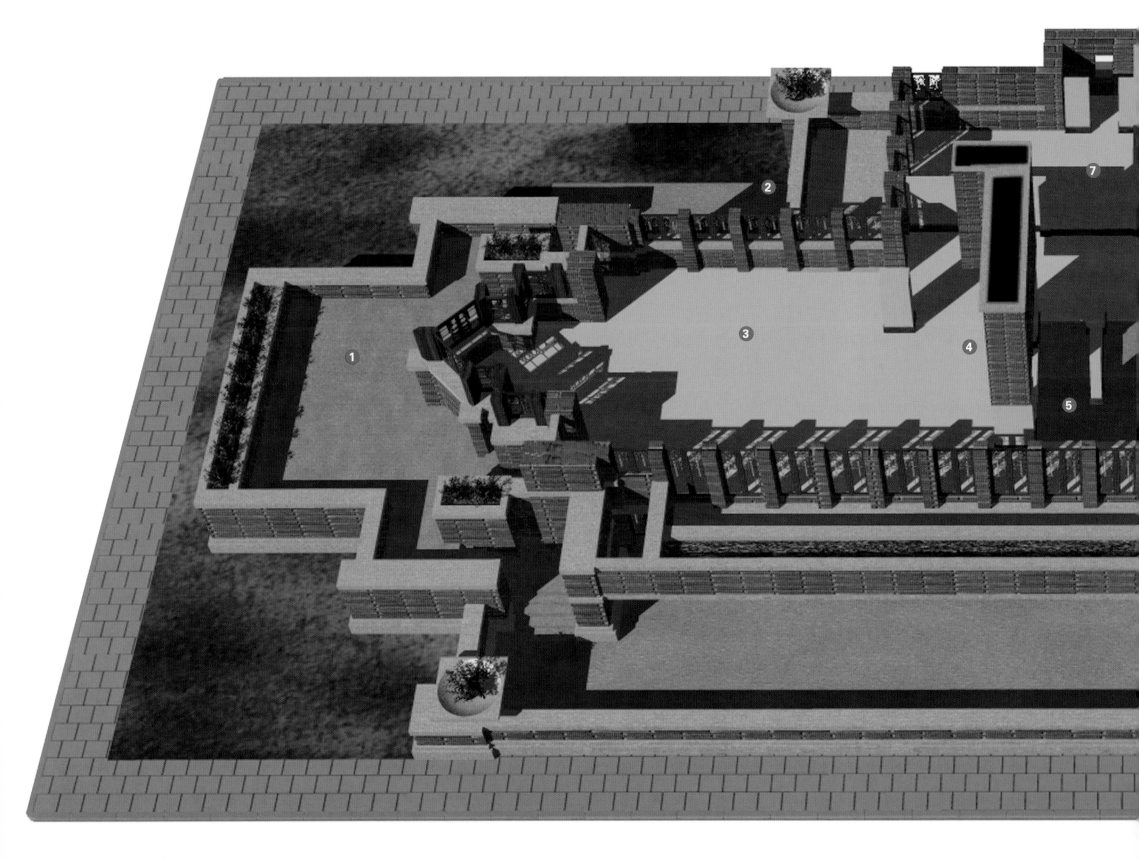

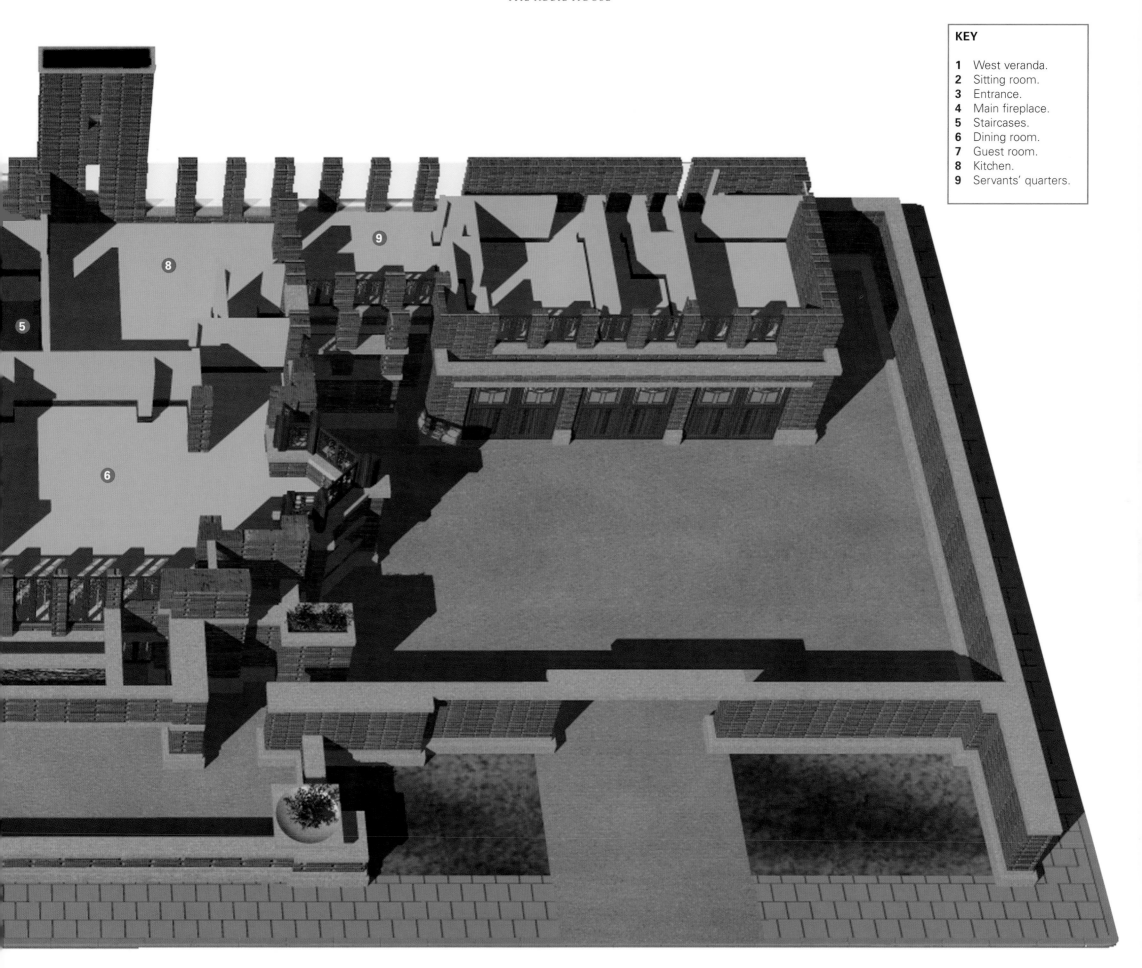

KEY

1 West veranda.
2 Sitting room.
3 Entrance.
4 Main fireplace.
5 Staircases.
6 Dining room.
7 Guest room.
8 Kitchen.
9 Servants' quarters.

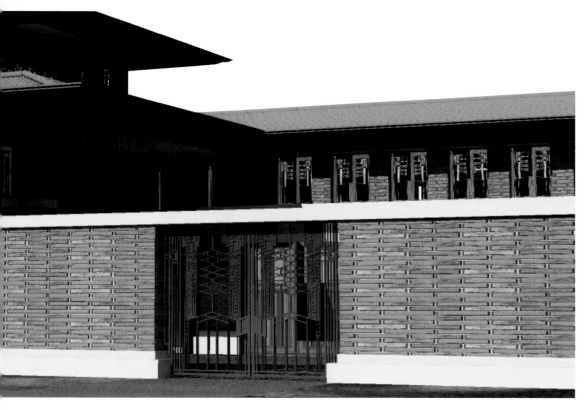

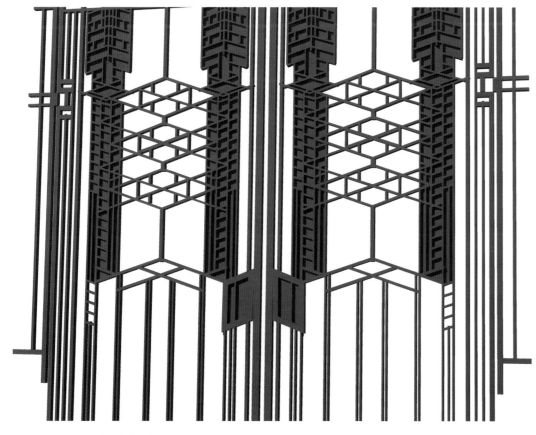

TOP AND ABOVE: *Wright designed the gates to allow cars access. They are in a stylized design of grain shafts and triangular shapes that echo the art-glass in the house.*

RIGHT: *The woodwork is a distinctive feature of the house. Unfortunately much of the cabinet work was badly damaged during the decline of the building and needs intensive restoration to conserve the pieces, this includes all the doors, radiator cabinets, and furniture.*

open to the public, consideration also had to be given to disability-access compliance, safety issues, and the effect of potentially huge numbers of visitors.

Once all the preliminary preparations had been made and plans drawn up, the first task was to stabilize the building by preventing further damage from water penetration and termite destruction-in one place damage was so extensive that a wall had to be taken down and replaced. The roof was repaired or rebuilt, masonry was repaired, and damaged bricks and limestone replaced. Much of the water damage was attributed to copper gutter linings that were not angled to drain properly. New liners were installed on the upper sections of all the gutters to rectify this, and as an additional precaution against leaks, an ice and water shield was installed.

Finding bricks to match those used by Wright involved a nationwide search that took a number of years. He had used Roman bricks, which were longer and narrower than most, flecked with iron spots and fired in a coal kiln. Eventually a compromise had to be reached by using Norman bricks. These are the same length as Roman but twice the height, so they were sliced horizontally in two.

Badly cracked plaster panels on the walls and ceilings were replaced with plaster matching the original composition and texture. All the internal electrical wiring was updated and a fire-detection system and dry-sprinkler system were installed. Installation of new mechanical systems, including state-of-the-art temperature and humidity controls, ensure a museum-quality interior environment, with all pipework and wiring concealed.

Restoration of the exterior and structure of the building constituted the first stage of the project, with the interior and detailing forming stage two. Plans included repairing and conserving 174 art glass (glass intended to make a decorative statement) windows; recreating the glass for the front door according to

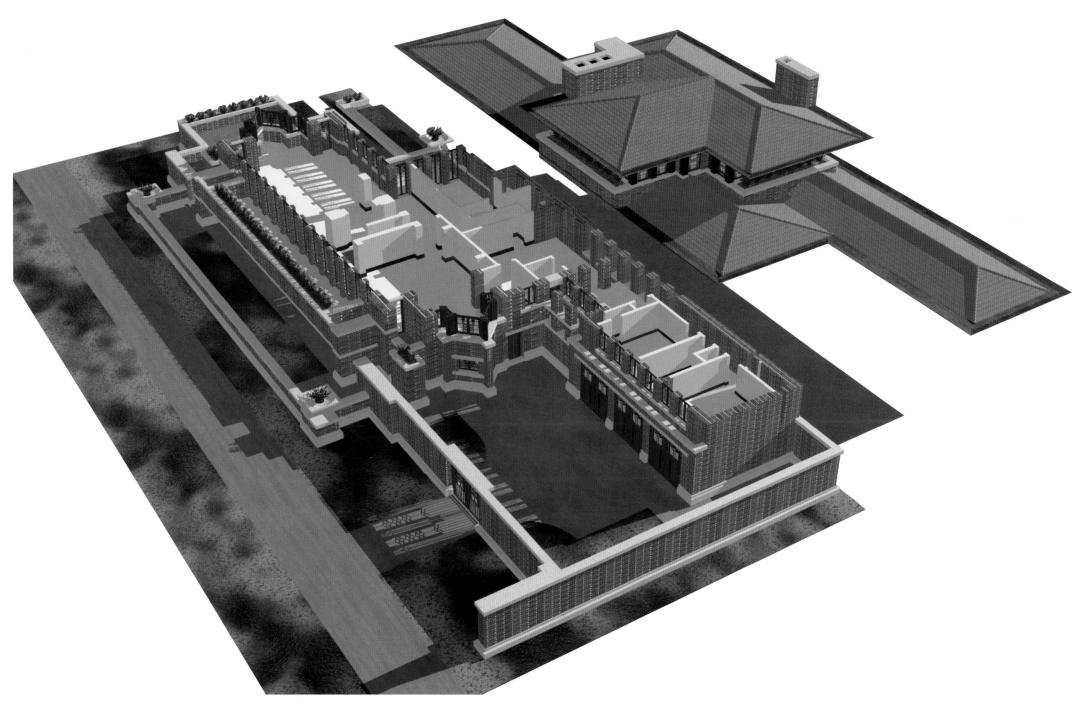

architectural drawings; making thirty-nine reproductions of bare bulb, square-shaped fixtures and twenty-five dome-shaped fixtures; and conserving thirty-two bronze sconces still in situ. Longer term it is hoped that furnishings, fabrics, fixtures, furniture, and decorative objects will be acquired, borrowed, or reproduced. Outside, landscaping and replanting of trees and shrubs has restored the house's original setting.

INFO

A book and gift shop is housed in the former garage. Guided and self-guided tours are available daily (except Thanksgiving, Christmas Day, and New Year's Day).

5757 Woodlawn Avenue, Chicago, Illinois 60637
www.wrightplus.org/robiehouse/robiehouse.html

ABOVE: *Graphic showing the main living areas without the roof and the top story. This emphasizes the central location of the fireplace—a key Wrightian theme—and the length of the sitting room.*

RIGHT: *By 1941 the Chicago Seminary considered the Robie House unusable and decided to demolish it. This was only prevented by the Committee for the Preservation of Robie House. In 1956–57, the Seminary tried again to get the building demolished. Wright decided to fight for his masterpiece and said, "To destroy it would be like destroying a great piece of sculpture or a great work of art. It would never be permitted in Europe. It could only happen in America, and it is particularly sad that professional religionists should be the executioners . . . It all goes to show the danger of entrusting anything spiritual to the clergy."*

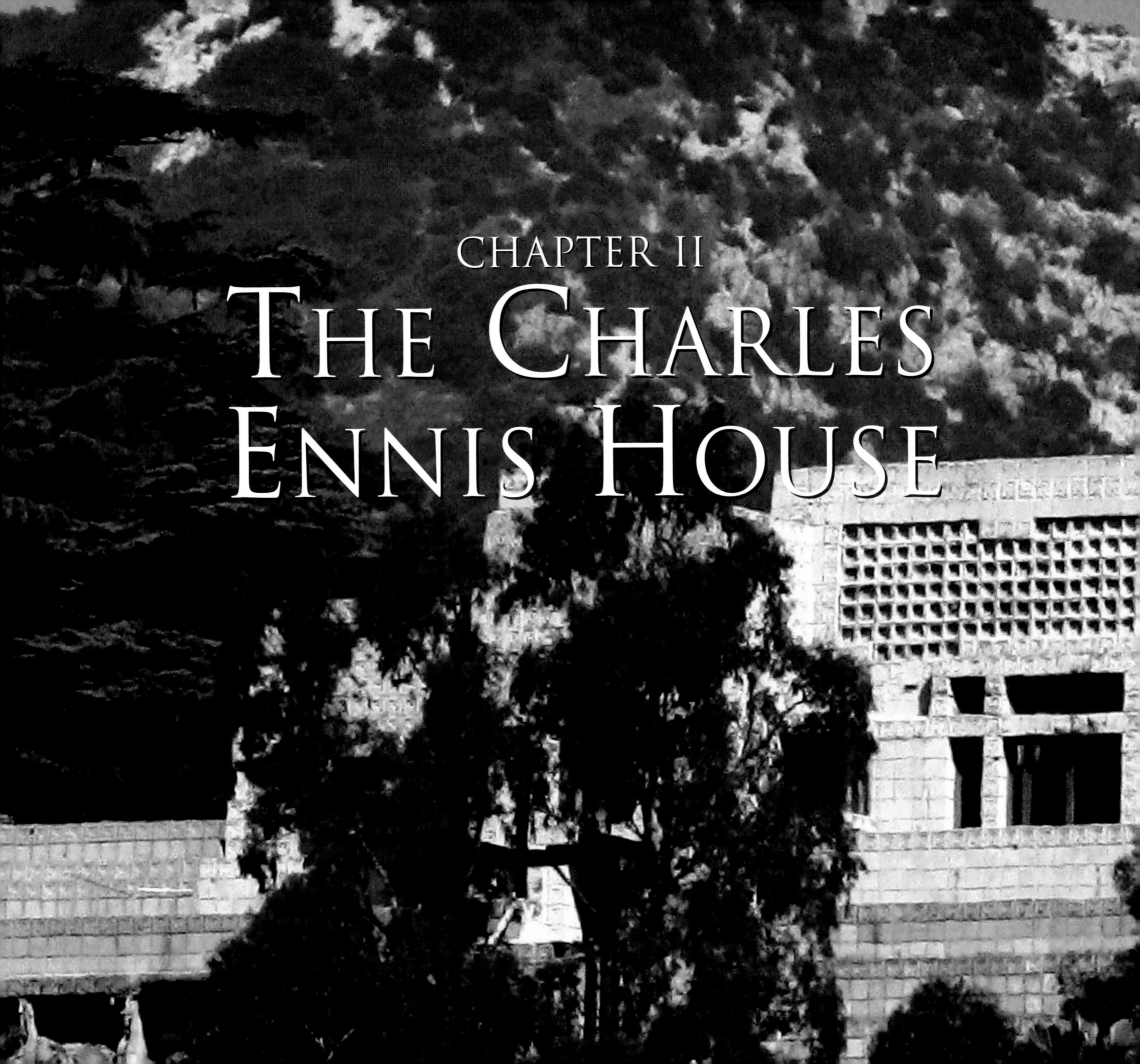

CHAPTER II

THE CHARLES ENNIS HOUSE

THE CHARLES ENNIS HOUSE

HISTORY

The Charles Ennis House, occupying a half-acre plot in the Loz Feliz area of Los Angeles, California, is the largest and grandest of what are known as Wright's concrete-block, or textile-block houses. From its ridge on the southern slopes of the Santa Monica Mountains it looks toward Griffith Park to the north and the Los Angeles metropolitan area to the south.

BELOW: *South face. The Ennis House is a City of Los Angeles Cultural Heritage Monument and a designated California State Landmark. It is also listed by the U.S. Department of the Interior in the National Register of Historic Places.*

When Wright finally returned in 1922 from prolonged stays in Japan, where he spent some time overseeing his design of the Imperial Hotel in Tokyo (his largest project up to that time), he decided to open a practice in Los Angeles. His first commission there, some years earlier (in 1917), had been Hollyhock House, built for oil heiress Aline Barnsdall. This house represented his first attempt to develop a style of architecture appropriate to southern California and shows his early experiments with surface texture. It also echoes the Mayan style Wright later used for the Ennis House. Hollyhock House (so named because it was Ms. Barnsdall's

favorite flower, and interpretations of the motif can be seen all around the house) was intended to form part of an arts-and-theater complex, but this was never completed. Aline Barnsdall donated Hollyhock House to the City of Los Angeles in 1927 and today it forms part of the Barnsdall Art Park, which includes an art gallery and a theater. On a clear day the house can be seen to the south from Ennis House.

Wright wanted to build houses that would fit into the sun-baked Californian landscape, in accordance with his belief that houses should grow and merge from and into their surroundings. To help achieve

this he wanted a building material that would echo the texture and colors of the land and suit the climate-and he wanted to devise a building system that would be appropriate to the landforms and culture of southern California. By now poured concrete was a common and economical building material and Wright used it to create his "concrete blocks" or "textile blocks." Wright was not the first architect to experiment with modular blocks, but his were distinguished by their surface patterning.

The first of his four textile-block houses, all built in 1923, was "La Miniatura" in Pasadena, a combined house

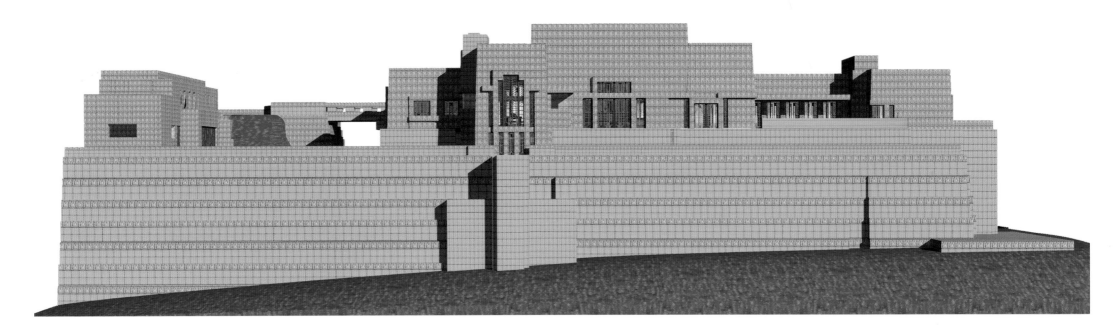

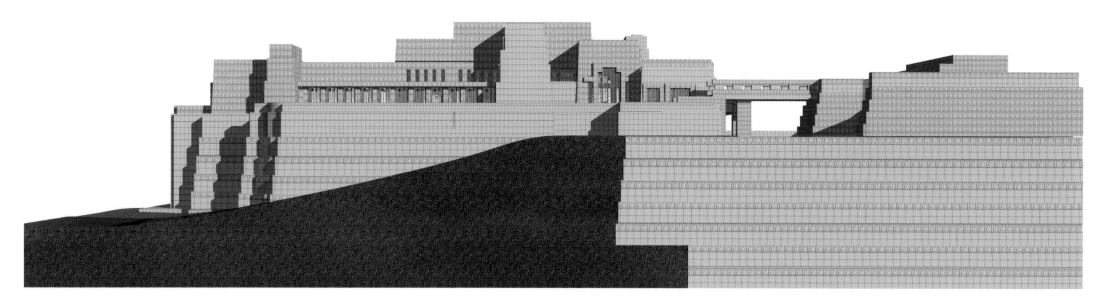

ABOVE: *The north elevation. The client, Mr. Charles Ennis was fascinated by the ancient Mayan culture and requested a house that reflected this interest. Wright, equally enamored with the Mesoamerican heritage, obliged with a design that has distinct echoes of Mayan temples with their elaborate carvings and reliefs.*

BELOW: *The northeast side. The Ennis House is situated high on the hill ridge in the Los Feliz neighborhood of north central Los Angeles, California. When it was built this was the most expensive and exclusive Los Angeles neighborhood.*

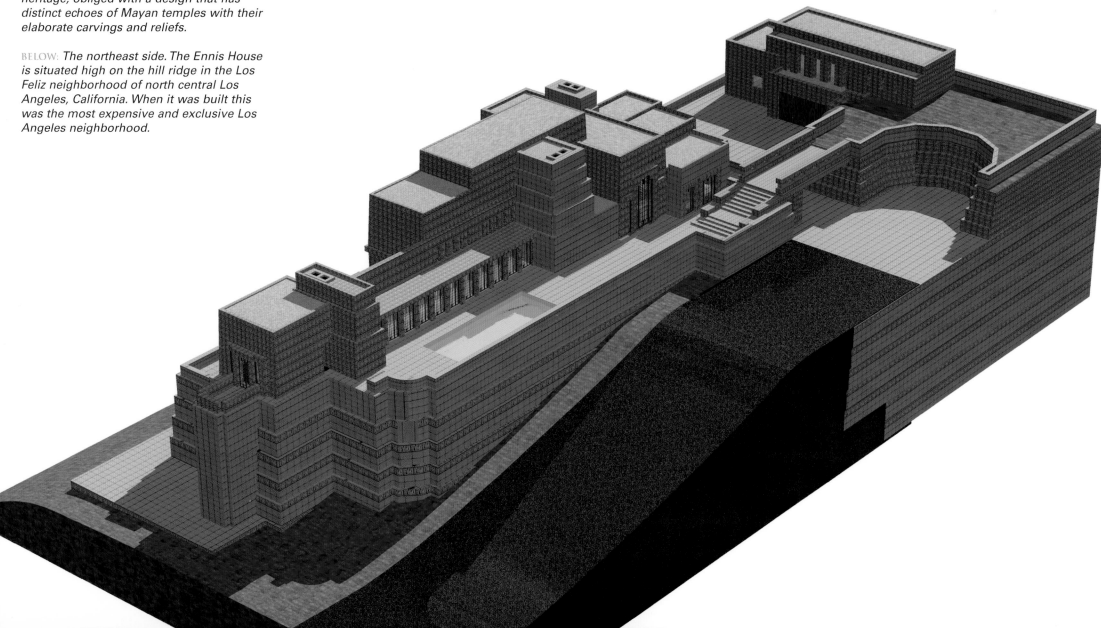

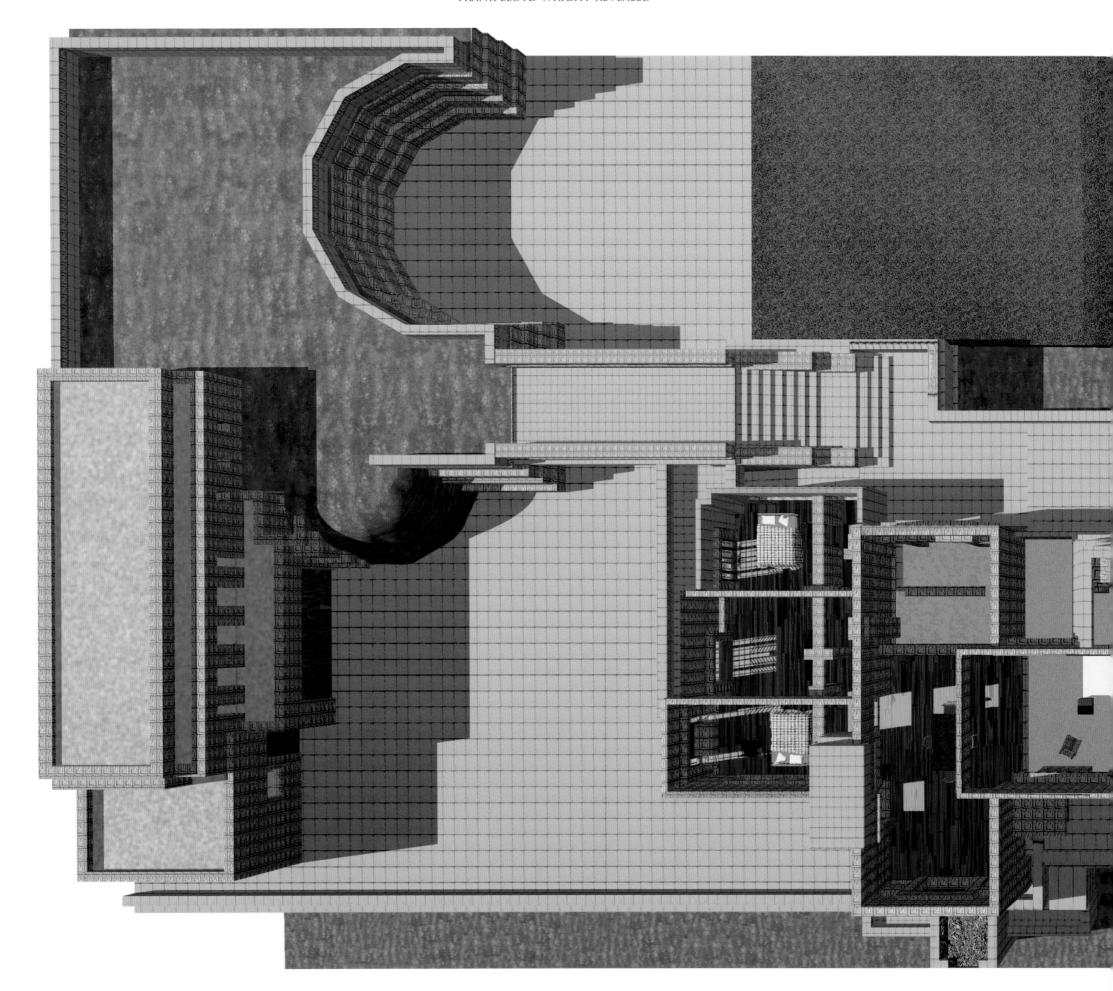

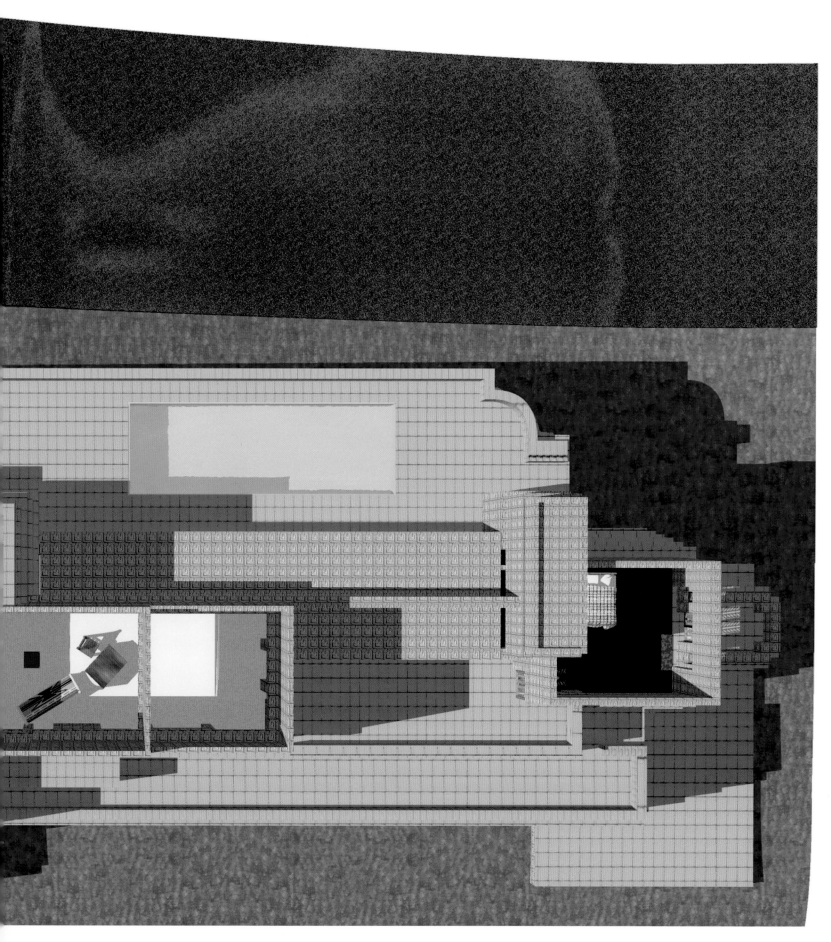

and book studio for Alice Millard (the widow of George Millard, a former client from Highland Park, near Chicago). Later Wright called it his first Usonian house. Here the two-story living room allows light in through "window walls" at the lower level and pierced, patterned blocks at the higher level. Designs recall the Mayan decorations at Oaxaca in Mexico.

The John Storer Residence, the second of the type to be built, also has a two-story living room, with one side opening up to spectacular views of the Hollywood hills. Most spectacular, however, is the living room of the Freeman Residence-the smallest of the four houses-which became a center of artistic and political activity in Los Angeles. In 1986 Harriet Freeman gave the house to the University of Southern California School of Architecture so that it would be protected and preserved. Here Wright used perforated blocks inset with glass and put the bedrooms below the living rooms. Damage from the Northbridge earthquake and the fragile nature of the blocks means the house, like Ennis House, is undergoing restoration.

Charles Ennis and his wife, Mabel, who had moved to Los Angles in about 1901 and opened a clothing store there, were inspired by Wright's houses and his reputation, and commissioned him to build their house in 1923. As leading members of L.A. society, they wanted a home that would impress their wealthy friends and incite comment.

Construction of the house began, but Wright and the Ennises fell out over matters of design and Wright left Lloyd Wright (1890-1978), the eldest of his seven children, who also became an architect, to supervise the construction of the house-as indeed he did for Wright's three other textile-block houses. Wright junior was also responsible for designing the landscaping

LEFT: *The plan of the roof clearly shows the ambition of both client and architect. The north terrace swimming pool and ground floor billiards room were added by the next owner, John Nesbitt, but designed by Wright.*

around all four houses. Shortly after, Wright, feeling that there was no future for him in California, returned to Taliesin West, in Arizona. Charles Ennis died in 1928 (the funeral was held in the house) and Mabel continued to live there until 1936.

In 1940 the house was bought by John Nesbitt (1910-60), a radio narrator and movie producer at MGM, for $20,000. Nesbitt invited Wright to work on the house again, a commission Wright was please to accept because to his mind it had never been completed to his precise instructions. The swimming pool on the north terrace was added, and a storage room on the ground floor was turned into a

billiards room. A forced-air heating system for the house-its first heating system-was also installed.

Mr. Augustus O. Brown and his wife, Marcia, bought the house in 1968. Mr. Brown, who is still on the board of trustees today, founded the Trust for Preservation of Cultural Heritage, a nonprofit organization, in 1980, to ensure the continued maintenance of the house. It was under their care that the house was renamed the Ennis-Brown House, but in August 2005 the name was changed back to the Charles Ennis House. During the Browns' ownership a bedroom and a bathroom added since the house was first built were

replaced with the garden, which had been there originally.

The house has also had a separate career on the silver screen, appearing in twenty or more films, as well as being used as a backdrop for music videos, commercials, and fashion shoots. Notable among the films is Blade Runner, a 1982 science fiction cult classic directed by Ridley Scot and starring Harrison Ford. The modified house is the home of Rick Deckard, the hunter of the humanoid robots, known as "replicants." Scott liked the house so much that he used it again in the crime drama Black Rain (1989). Its most famous role, however, is probably as

the mansion in the 1959 horror movie starring Vincent Price, House on Haunted Hill, which provided the inspiration for Alfred Hitchcock's 1960 classic, Psycho.

The income from the house's use in films and the increase of visitors as a result of it being seen on screen has contributed considerably to its upkeep over the years.

THE HOUSE DESCRIBED
The starting point for the design of the house was Ennis' and Wright's shared love of the architecture of the Mayan civilization of South America, which flourished in different phases from about 250 BC to the Spanish Conquest in the midsixteenth

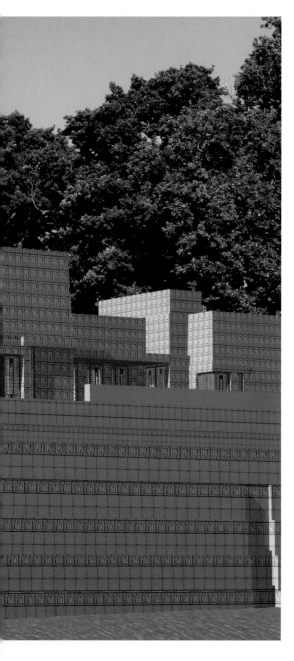

ABOVE: *The main approach. Frank Lloyd Wright designed the house for Charles and Mabel Ennis in 1923 in Mesoamerican style and it was built the following year.*

ABOVE RIGHT: *The metalwork in the house is based on Mayan imagery and motifs. It is known that Wright did not design these features although they appear throughout the building—on escutcheons, in light switches, and lock plates, as well as the magnificent iron gate at the entrance.*

RIGHT: *The entrance to the house lies below the main level of the building.*

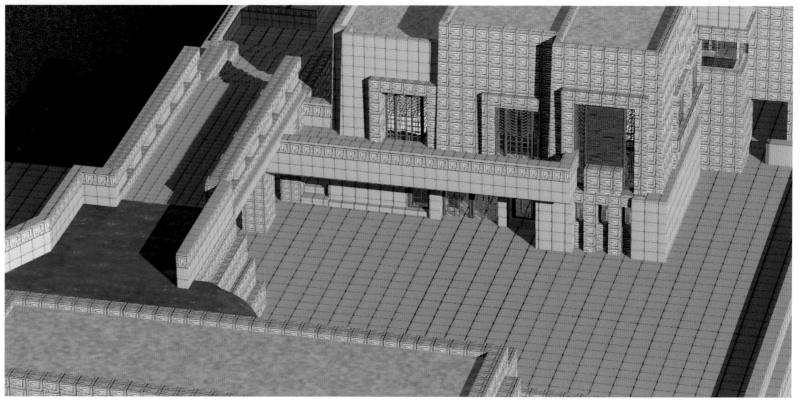

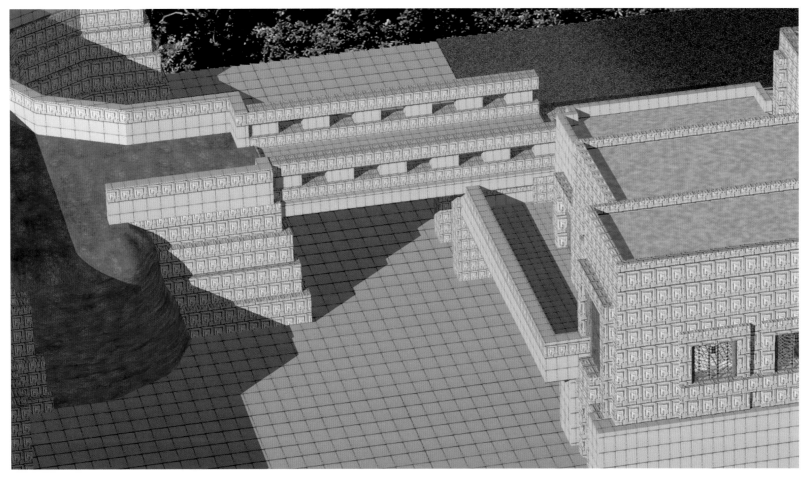

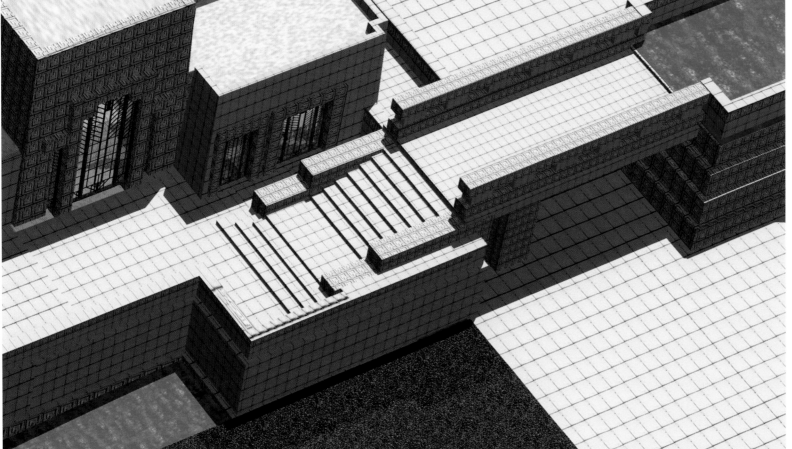

TOP LEFT AND LEFT: *Bridge and courtyard.*

ABOVE: *Courtyard entrance.*

FOLLOWING PAGE: *The poor condition of the building is only too apparent—the textile blocks are decaying and plants grow out of the masonry. At some time in the past a previous owner had applied a poor quality waterproofing sealant to the blocks; but where the grout had been badly applied water seeped in and instead of drying out as before, the sealant trapped the moisture which in turn rusted the iron strengthening bars and damaged the blocks. This makes restoration much trickier.*

century. The monumental Mayan buildings, mostly limestone structures faced with stucco, were characterized by elaborately carved surfaces and friezes, stepped pyramids, sloping facades, and hidden doorways-all elements that can be seen interpreted in the Ennis House.

On approaching the house from the north, the massive building comprised of huge blocks seems too big for its site. (Later Wright admitted that it was too big for a concrete-block house.) Flat-roofed and with no clear definition of levels or shape,

its position along the top of the ridge, with its main facade rising almost sheer from the steep slope, immediately gives the 248-foot-long building an imposing, defensive presence. Relatively few windows, set up high, on this side accentuate its resemblance to a fortress. Wright's personal life was in turmoil at this time and the house could have reflected the seclusion and solitude he sought.

The basic unit of the concrete blocks Wright created for his California houses was a sixteen-inch-square tile of cast

concrete just a little under four inches thick. On all four edges semicircular grooves were hollowed out so steel reinforcing rods could be inserted into both the vertical and horizontal joints to create a structural grid, a concrete "fabric" that could be used for floors, ceilings, and walls both inside and out. There were no visible mortar lines and the seams were filled with liquid concrete, giving the massed effect that echoes the solidity of the adobe houses of the Pueblo Indians of New Mexico and Arizona.

When the walls were constructed,

two layers of blocks were often used, leaving a space in between for insulation. The blocks were cast on site, incorporating sand and crushed stone whenever possible to replicate the surrounding soil and rock and to bring about the organic effect Wright strove for. Very little skilled labor was needed to make the blocks—in theory, one man could handle them keeping costs down. In reality the unevenness of the blocks and problems with construction meant they turned out quite expensive.

Into these blocks it was possible to

stamp designs on both sides, creating patterns that could then be repeated all over the surfaces of the building, both inside and out. Tiles were rotated to produce different effects and some were left blank to provide contrast. Wright named these "textile" blocks because he saw the steel as the warp and the masonry squares as the woof, with himself as the weaver, creating textures and patterns that emulated both the decorations on pre-Columbian architecture and recalled the crafts of indigenous cultures. The blocks for each of the four Californian houses were cast with their own signature geometric design. As it turned out they were all for wealthy clients, but the idea of module design was a recurring theme in Wright's work from then on, driven by his quest for mass-production.

Entry to the house is via a covered entrance below the main level at the western end of the building. Wrought-iron gates lead into a courtyard bounded by the house on one side and the separate double garage and chauffeur's quarters on the other (planning permission for this block had to be applied for separately). From here there are wide views of the hills to the south. The bridge above the gates links the garden on the north side of the house with a smaller garden to the northwest of the courtyard.

To the left of the courtyard low, squat, patterned concrete pillars announce the doorway to the lower level of the house. From there a dark, twisting, low-ceilinged passage leads up stairs to the 100-foot loggia that stretches along the entire north front of the house at first-floor level, its twenty pairs of square, concrete-block pillars standing to attention. It is probably the longest Wright ever designed. Used as an extension of the living space, this "hallway" links (from west to east) the dining room, the living room-where it becomes part of the room, screening off the fireplace and the outer windows step up a half-story-and the two principal bedrooms, which are separated by a large terrace.

Reached from the western end of

LEFT: *The southwest facade and dining room.*

RIGHT: *The interior of the dining room. Wright devised the textile-block system as a way of using inexpensive materials such as concrete to create a unique and individual feel for every house. Each house had its own textile-block pattern which was used throughout the exterior and interior.*

BELOW: *The balcony below the dining room window. The concrete blocks are 16in square and decorated with geometric repeat patterns. Placed one on top of the other they create a rich textural finish on what would otherwise be a dull concrete wall. Architects were dismissive of the aesthetics of concrete, but Frank Lloyd Wright responded— "they lived mostly in the architectural gutter as an imitation of rock-faced stone. Why not see what could be done with that gutter rat?" — and proved his point with his textile-block houses.*

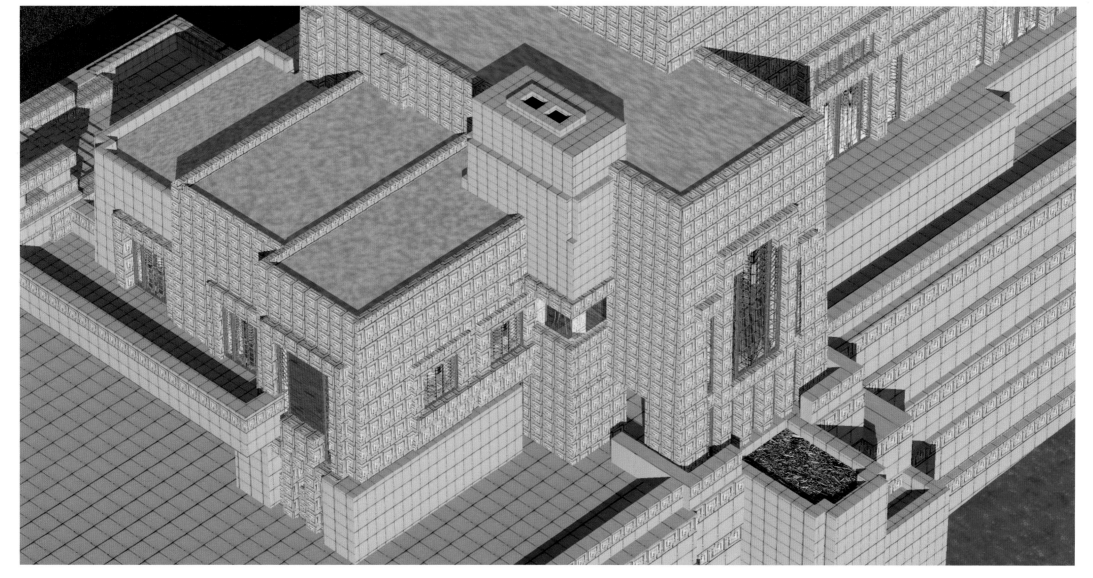

ABOVE: *The monochromatic interiors are enlivened by sophisticated art glass in the form of abstract wisteria blossoms. The glass in the windows and doors graduates in* *intensity from dark at the top to lighter at the bottom. After the Ennis House Wright did not include art glass in his domestic buildings.*

RIGHT: *The Tiffany hearth. Wright only designed four art-glass mosaics. One is in the Ennis House above the living room fireplace and shows a twist of wisteria.*

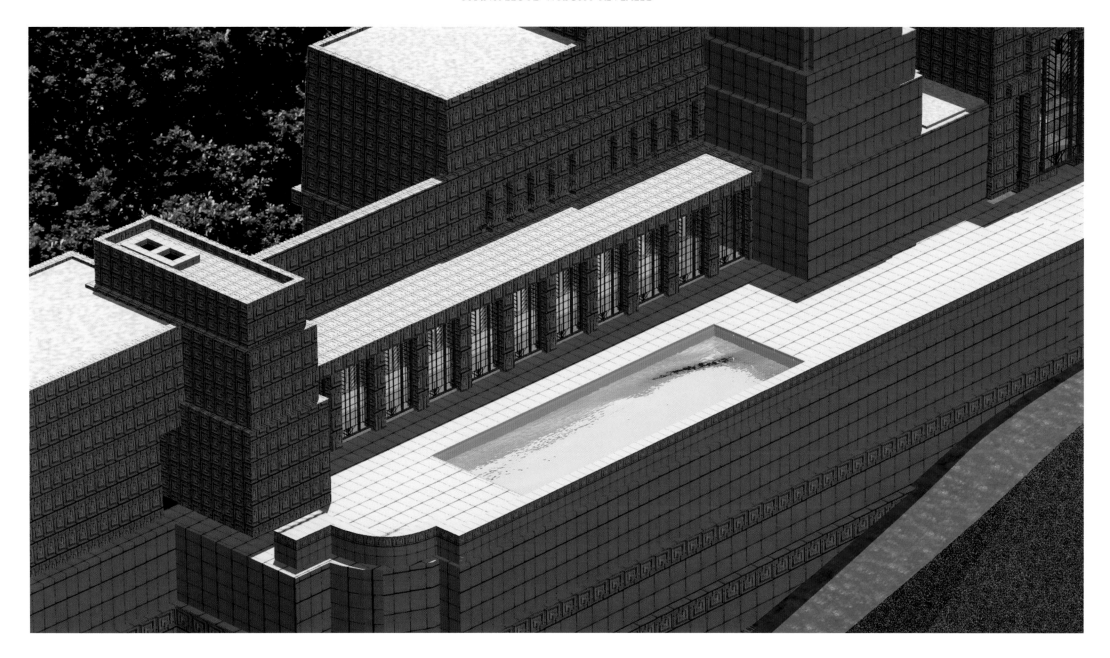

the loggia, up a few steps, is the dining room, which projects out from the rest of the house to the south. It is set up higher than the living room, from which it is separated by a low wall. Wooden floorboards align with the direction of the beams on the wooden ceiling. A tall, triple-section art-glass window looks out toward the city and a fireplace is recessed into the decorated concrete blocks that make up the walls. On the south side of the room are examples of Wright's mitered corner windows. Next to the dining room, at the same level on the west side, is the kitchen, a pantry, and a guest room, placed one behind the other.

A short flight of steps leads down from the dining room into the living area. Anyone who has watched the film Blade Runner may be able to identify parts of these two rooms, which were used to make up Deckard's apartments. The twenty-two-foot-high living room is formal and hall-like, on a scale in keeping with the ostentation and wealth of Hollywood society. Wright referred to it as the "Great Room." There is nothing cozy or homey about it and it is difficult to imagine anyone living there. The fireplace-as always in Wright's living areas-is a significant feature, but set behind the columns of the loggia as it is, does not dominate the room. A large, striking glass mosaic above the fire grate depicts a wisteria tree set against a

ABOVE: *The north terrace pool and colonnade. The swimming pool was added in 1940 by radio personality John Nesbitt for which he commissioned Frank Lloyd Wright. At the same time he also added a ground floor billiards room and a forced air heating system for the house.*

RIGHT: *Such a sun loving and extravagant building suits the arid, open environment of Southern California beautifully. As Wright matured as an architect his views as to what a building should be and how it should present itself also evolved. One of Wright's lifelong precepts was that a building should fit into its surroundings as naturally as possible. This meant, among other things, an integrity with the landscape achieved through the use of local materials wherever possible.*

RIGHT AND BELOW RIGHT: *The colonnade and terrace. A great advantage of the textile-block system was that it could be cast and made on site by unskilled labor. Although hugely extravagant in his personal tastes, Wright was very conscious of making affordable housing and was pleased with the possibilities of pre-cast concrete blocks.*

background of gold tiles that reflect the light. Orlando Giannini (1861-1928), an art-glass maker from Chicago, who had worked with Wright before, executed Wright's design. On the right-hand side of the fireplace a tall, narrow cupboard-more than twelve feet high-was designed to store ladders, presumably so the clerestory windows on either side of the fireplace could be reached.

In these two rooms the floors, ceilings and door and window frames of polished teak contrast with the lighter wall blocks. This choice of wood by the Ennises was one of the many things that they and Wright disagreed on: Wright wanted to use redwood, always preferring the native resources. He also wanted slate for the floor of the loggia, but the owners insisted on marble. Other introductions by the Ennises included all the metalwork (for example, the wrought-iron entrance gates and window grills, the copper fireplace hood in the dining room), which was made by Julius Dietzman, a local craftsman, and the chandeliers in the loggia. What eventually caused Wright to walk out, though, was the owners' wish to alter his design of the living room and the dining room.

A balcony on the south side of the living room looks over the lower terrace, and the art-glass doors to the right lead to the bedroom used by Mabel Ennis. Charles Ennis's bedroom, across the garden terrace, is the only bedroom with a fireplace. Both rooms have full-length windows.

Ennis House features more art glass than Wright's other textile-block houses and they were the last pieces Wright designed for a domestic building. The geometric

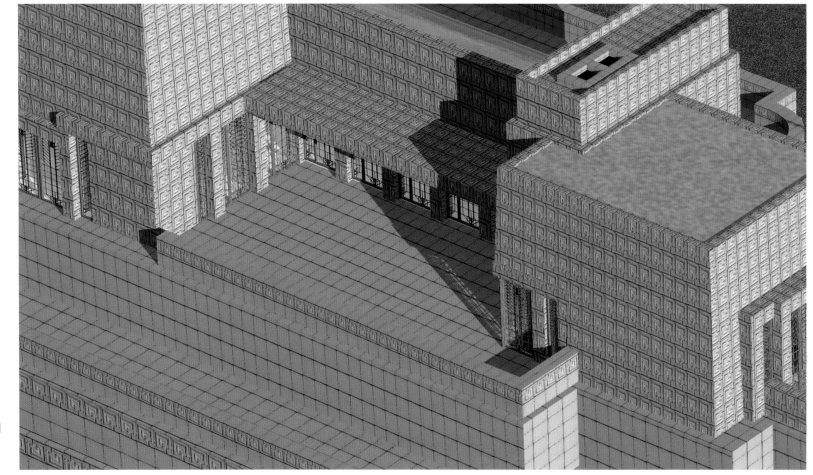

LEFT: *The colonnade. Each textile block is reinforced with steel rods cast inside the joint. The blocks are cast in molds to produce a 3in-thick, 16in-square block with decoration on both sides. They are then assembled one on top of the other with no visible mortar joints. Thin concrete and steel reinforcing rods run vertically and horizontally through the blocks to knit them together. The cavity air space between the blocks serves as insulation.*

ABOVE: *The south facade and dining room. The block pattern on the Ennis House is symmetrical around the diagonal of its square surface, and is different from Frank Lloyd Wright's three other California textile-block homes.*

ABOVE: *Staircase. The atmospheric qualities of the Ennis House have been seen in the movies* House on Haunted Hill, Blade Runner, Rush Hour, Black Rain, The Rocketeer, *and* The Thirteenth Floor, *among many others.*

RIGHT: *The house has also appeared on TV, most notably it was occupied by vampires in* Buffy the Vampire Slayer. *It has also been the backdrop for many commercials and music videos.*

INTERNAL VIEWS: *Although on the exterior many of the textile blocks have not worn well over the years and lost their characteristic detailing, the interior blocks are still in good condition. Teak is used extensively throughout the interior for doors, floors, windows, and furniture.*

BELOW: *The Ennis House became known as the Ennis-Brown House in 1980 in recognition of the work done by owner (1968–80) Augustus O. Brown who donated the house to the non-profit Trust for Preservation of Cultural Heritage; but in August 2005 the name was reverted back to Ennis House.*

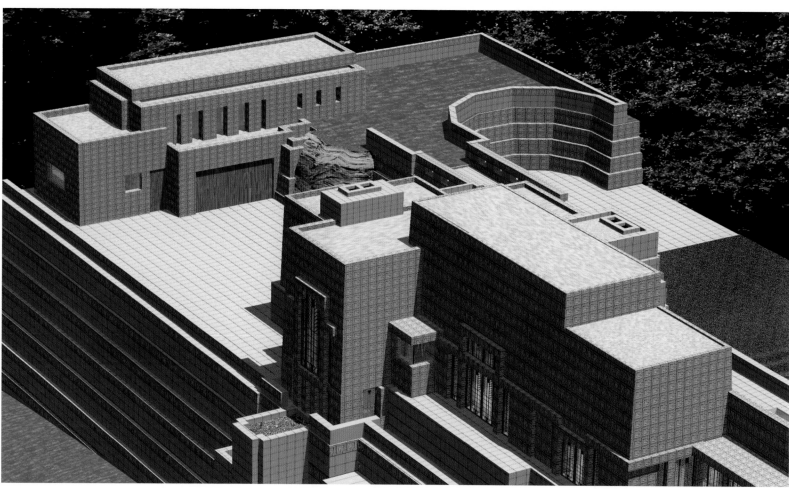

LEFT: *The interior stairway. The dramatic play of light and shade on the textile blocks has made the Ennis House a favorite location for movie directors with over 20 movies.*

ABOVE: *Garage, east view. Already in a state of serious decay the house was further badly damaged in the 1994 Northridge Earthquake. The retaining wall failed following the rainstorms of winter 2004 and further damaged by heavy rains in March 2006. Happily the funds have now been raised to restore it.*

patterns recall some of the earlier designs he used in his Prairie-style houses, although some of the motifs may have been derived from the pine trees in the garden on the north side of the house.

During Nesbitt's ownership Wright designed a range of furniture for the house that he named "Sijistan," after a Persian hero, but this was never made.

TODAY

Ennis House has not stood up well to the test of time and in 2005 was one of the National Trust for Historic Preservation's eleven most endangered sites, a list that was devised to raise awareness about the dangers to America's heritage. It is also on the World Monuments Fund list of the 100 most endangered sites in the world.

Deterioration of the house has come about through neglect, ill-advised repairs by previous owners, age and natural disasters. Los Angeles's renowned air-pollution, causing damage to the fragile concrete

blocks, has been another significant contributory factor.

At one time a sealant was painted onto the outside of the walls, trapping water inside that has rusted the steel reinforcing bars and caused the blocks to crack and splinter in places. As a result of the devastating earthquake that shook Los Angeles on January 17, 1994, the south retaining wall collapsed, as did the chauffeur's rooms and the structural support for the dining room. In January and February 2005 a series of torrential rainstorms left much of southern California waterlogged and hillsides vulnerable to mudslides. During these storms considerable damage was done to the house's retaining wall and west terrace, as well as to the roof and much of the interior. Conditions were so bad that in the March the City of Los Angeles declared the house uninhabitable and unsafe by red-tagging it (meaning no entry). While the building's emergency status has since been changed

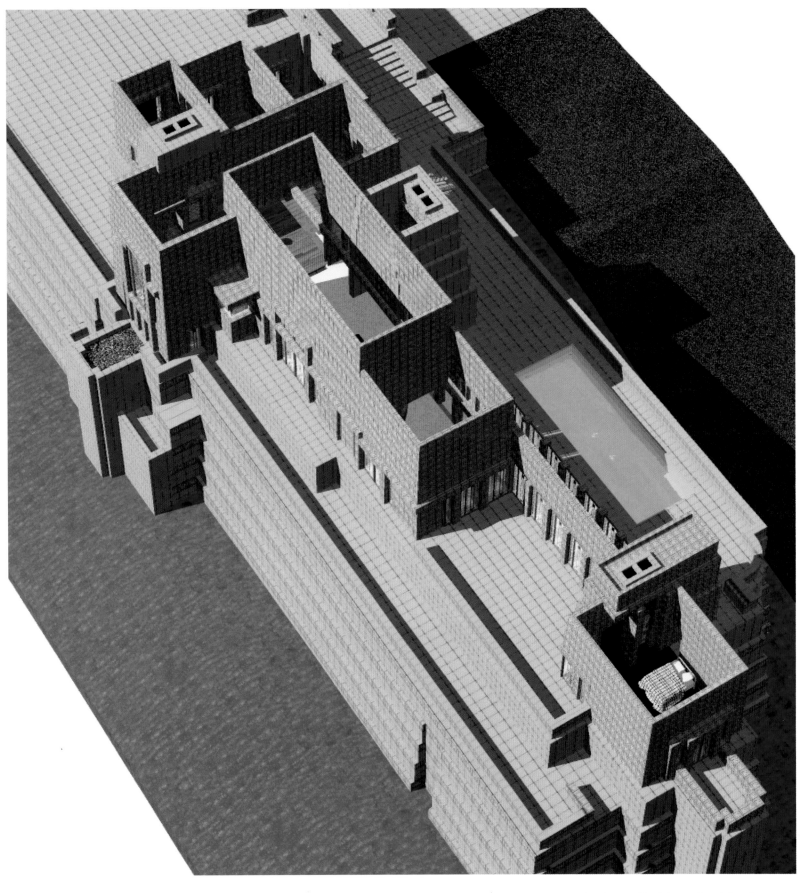

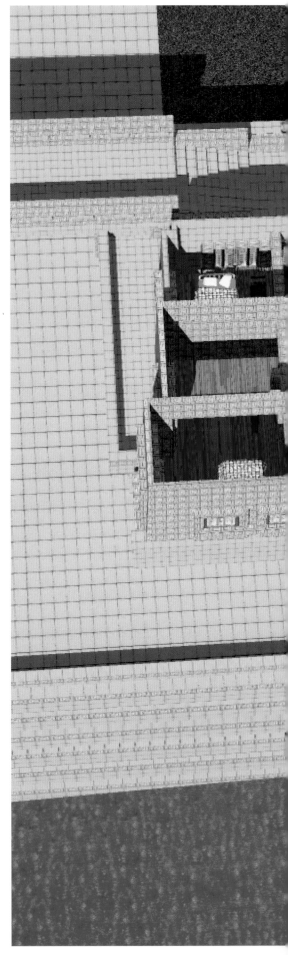

ABOVE AND RIGHT: *Two views of the roof levels. The Ennis House was the fourth and easily biggest of Frank Lloyd Wright's famous Southern California textile-block houses and* *was completed in 1924 with later additions in 1923 and again in 1940. His other textile-block commissions are Millard House (La Miniatura) for Alice Millard in Pasadena in* *1923; the Storer Residence for John Storer in Hollywood in 1923; and the Freeman Residence for Harriet and Samuel Freeman in Los Angeles in 1923.*

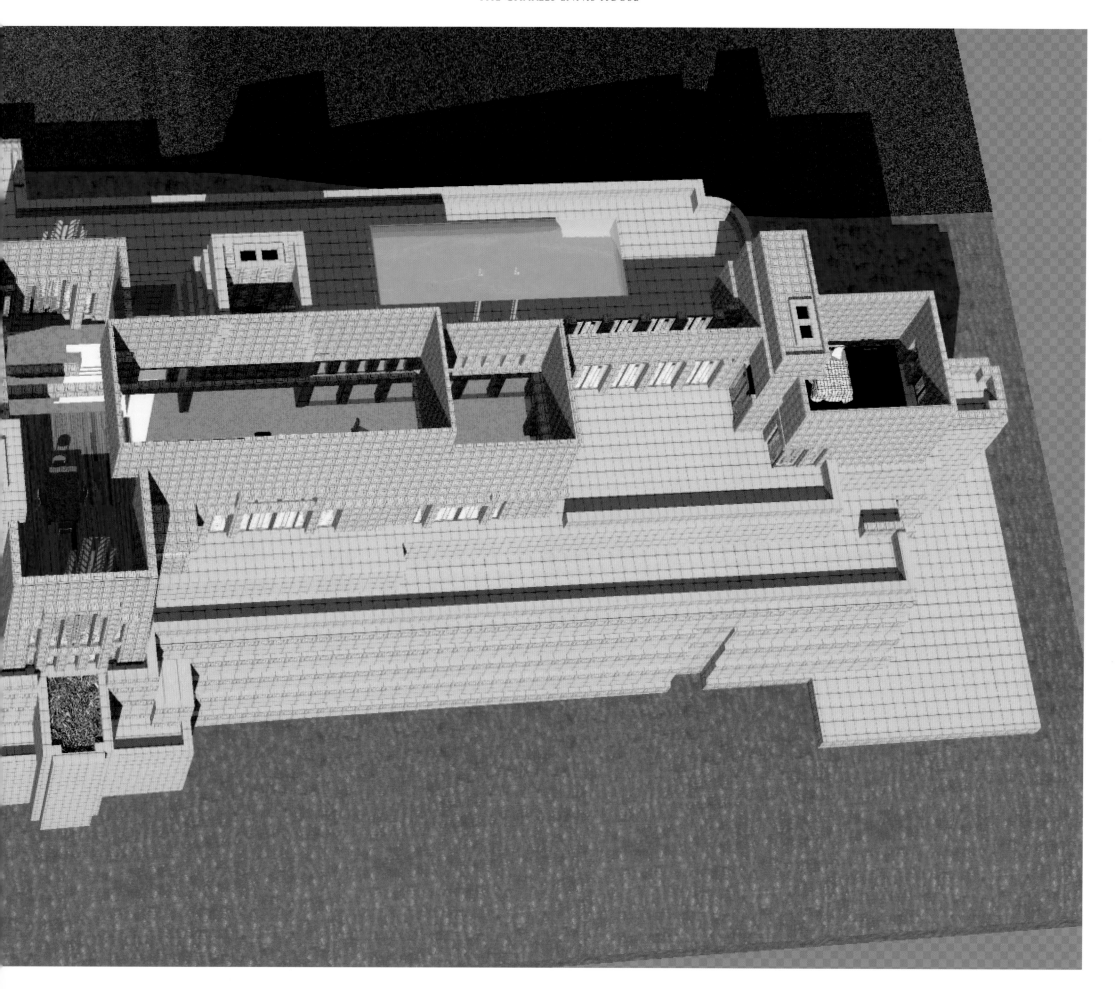

ABOVE: *The view from the living room through the art glass windows looks out over the Loz Felix area of Los Angeles.*

RIGHT: *Much of the furniture was specially designed for the Ennis House—here the table and chairs are made from teak embellished with art deco copper panel detailing.*

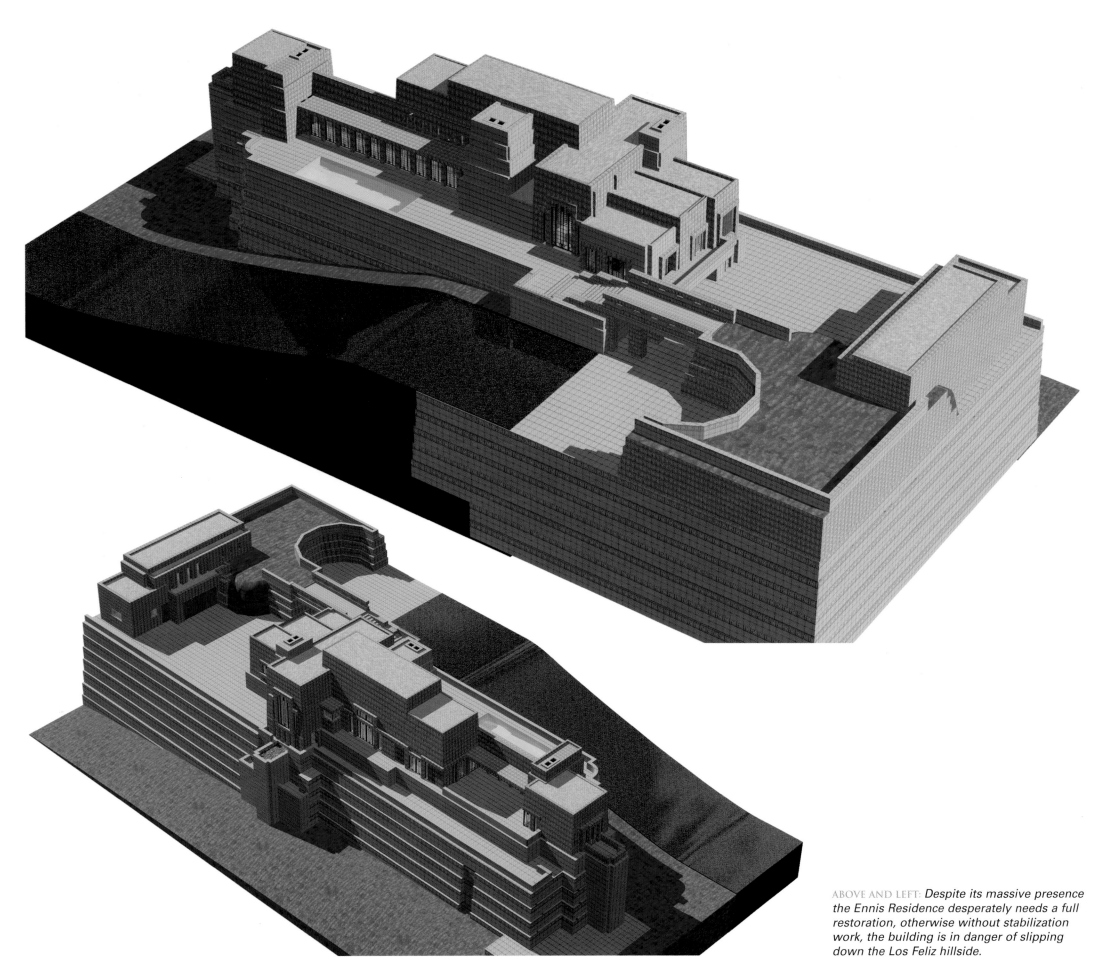

ABOVE AND LEFT: *Despite its massive presence the Ennis Residence desperately needs a full restoration, otherwise without stabilization work, the building is in danger of slipping down the Los Feliz hillside.*

to a yellow tag (meaning limited entry), urgent measures are imperative. Further rain will exacerbate the damage.

The Ennis House Foundation (formerly known as the Trust for Preservation of Cultural Heritage), which now owns and operates the site as a museum, the Los Angeles Conservancy, the National Trust for Historic Preservation, and the Frank Lloyd Wright Conservancy are all uniting to raise the funds needed for structural stabilization and repairs. Actress Diane Keaton is one of the supporters of the campaign. The amount needed is thought to be in the region of $5 million for structural repairs alone, with a further $15 million required for full restoration. The foundation has already been awarded a $2 million grant from the FEMA (Federal Emergency Management Agency).

Wright's grandson (son of Lloyd Wright Jr.) Eric Lloyd Wright and a team of specialists have been enlisted by the Foundation to oversee the house's restoration and preservation. Eric was a student at Taliesin, in Arizona, and he has restored and renovated a number of his grandfather's and father's works, as well as executing his own designs. He is also the founder of the Wright Way Organic Resource Center in Malibu, California.

RIGHT: *The outer retaining wall was damaged by heavy rains in March 2005.*

INFO

The house is listed by the U.S. Department of the Interior in the National Register of Historic Places, it has been declared a Cultural Heritage Monument by the City of Los Angeles, and has been designated a California State Landmark. Tours are available.

2655 Glendower Avenue, Los Angeles, www.ennishouse.org/htmls/textileblocks.htm

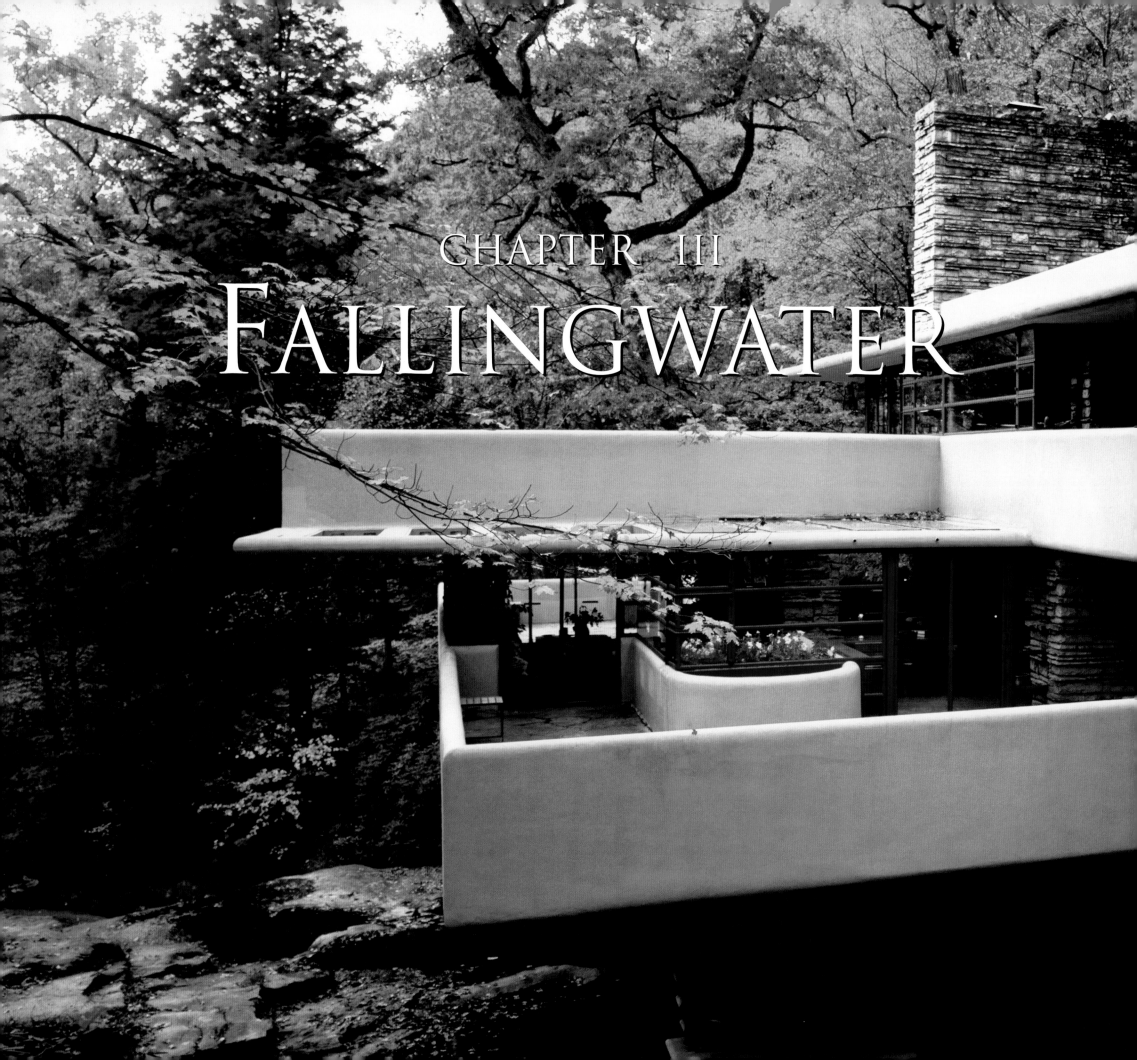

CHAPTER III
FALLINGWATER

FALLINGWATER

ABOVE: *Fallingwater almost disappears into the landscape in winter—just as Frank Lloyd Wright intended. He had very profound views about the relationship between building and landscape and always designed his structures to merge with their surroundings with the sympathetic use of local materials and a sensitive appreciation of the forms of the land. Each of his projects was designed for its particular plot.*

HISTORY

Claimed in 1991 by members of the American Institute of Architects to be "the best all-time work of American architecture," the house known as Fallingwater epitomizes Frank Lloyd Wright's notion that buildings should merge seamlessly into their natural surroundings to present a unified, harmonious whole-to become one with the landscape and allow people to live with nature. It is probably Wright's most famous private house and draws thousands of visitors from all over the world every year.

The house stands on Bear Run, a creek in the Appalachian Mountains of Fayette County, western Pennsylvania. It is about two hours southeast of Pittsburgh, halfway between the villages of Mill Run and Ohiopyle. Adjacent is the five thousand-acre Bear Run Nature Reserve, with pine woods, rhododendron groves, oak woods, streams, waterfalls, marked walking trails, and outdoor activities. The reserve, along with the house, belongs to the Western Pennsylvania Conservancy.

Also known as the Kaufmann House, Fallingwater was conceived in 1935 for Edgar Kaufmann, owner of the Kaufmann Department Store of Pittsburgh. He had founded the store with his three brothers in the 1870s. Edgar was a man of charismatic charm and wide-ranging interests, of which architecture was one. As well as being a successful businessman

he was a patron of the arts. After marrying his first cousin, Lillian (she changed her name to the more elegant form of Liliane in the 1920s), the couple became celebrated society hosts and active in Pittsburgh affairs. They had long been familiar with the Bear Run area and in 1921 had a primitive log cabin built to the southeast of the falls (their favorite spot) on which Fallingwater stands and retreated to it whenever possible. In 1933 they bought several hundred acres along the river with a view to building a more substantial summer home right by the waterfall.

Meanwhile the Kaufmanns twenty-five-year-old son, Edgar Kaufmann Jr., had met Wright at Taliesin West, in Scottsdale, Arizona. Taliesin (meaning "shining brow" in Welsh, the language of Wright's forebears on his mother's side) was both Wright's West Coast home and a school for young apprentices. Kaufmann Jr. was one of these students, and on a visit to their son in his first year, 1934, Mr. and Mrs. Kaufmann met Wright and his third wife, Oligvanna. The two couples immediately hit it off and the occasion marked the beginning of a successful friendship and partnership that lasted until Wright's death in 1959. Over this period Kauffman commissioned Wright to design about six other projects and often came to the rescue of the Taliesin Fellowship when it ran into financial difficulties.

Later in 1934, at Edgar Jr.'s

RIGHT: *The northern elevation. Fallingwater was designed in 1935 for Edgar J Kaufmann and family to use as a weekend retreat from city life.*

BELOW: *Eastern elevation. Fallingwater became famous even before it was finished as people marvelled at its integrity with its surroundings and Wright's inspired ability to harmonize his building with the surroundings.*

ABOVE: *Western elevation. The Kaufmann family loved the waterfall on Bear Run and wanted their holiday home situated near it. Mr Kaufmann had not expected to live directly over the waterfall, that was entirely Wright's inspiration.*

LEFT: *Southern elevation. Fallingwater was passed on to Edgar J Kaufmann, jr in the 1950s. He was a curator at the Museum of Modern Art in New York and continued to use Fallingwater as a holiday retreat. He presented Fallingwater to the Western Pennsylvania Conservancy along with 1,543 acres of surrounding land on October 29, 1963.*

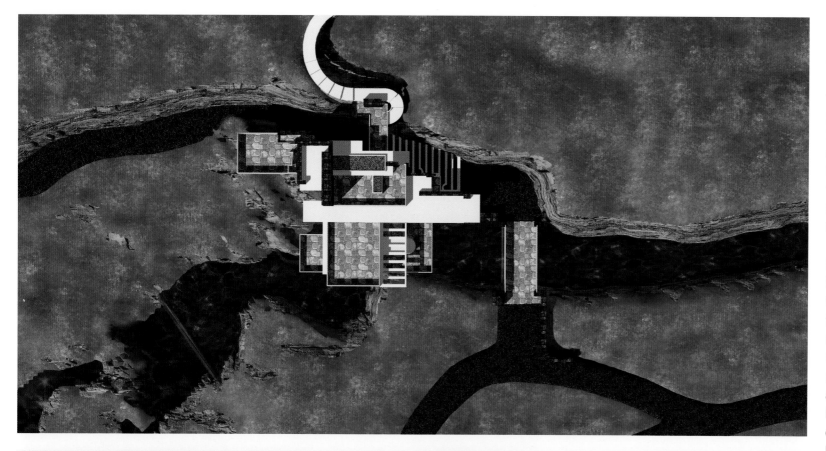

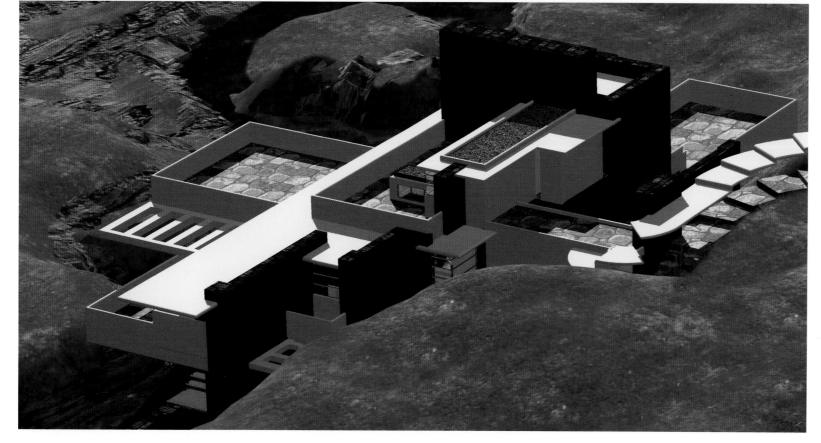

LEFT: *The house is anchored to the rocks and fits into the contours of the land like a glove. The jutting ledges are counterweighted by their mass at the rock face.*

TOP: *Aerial view. Building work started in 1936 and ended three years later with the completion of the guest house extension in 1939.*

ABOVE: *The north east corner. To maximize its local integrity Wright used local craftsmen and local materials in the construction of the house.*

suggestion, Wright visited the Kaufmanns in Pittsburgh. They took him to Bear Run and commissioned him to design their new house there and then. Immediately taken with the site, Wright knew that he would position the house over the falls, not looking up at them, which was the more obvious position and what the Kaufmanns had envisaged. He wanted the occupants to feel part of the ravine and for the relationship between house and setting to be almost symbiotic.

Kaufmann sent Wright a site survey in March 1935 and advised him that the cost-including furnishings-should be no more than $30,000. It was to be some months, though, before Wright put pen to paper and even then it seems his hand was forced. Kaufmann Senior telephoned Wright unexpectedly in September 1935 and announced that as he was only a few hours' drive away in Milwaukee he would drop by Taliesin to see how the plans for his house were coming along. Without missing a beat, Wright apparently intimated that that was no problem and promptly got out his drawing pencils and finished the plans as Kaufmann arrived about three hours later. This may or may not be entirely true, but it was certainly typical of Wright to let ideas evolve in his head for a long time then put them down swiftly, almost complete, in one go. Kaufmann approved the tidied-up plans in October and construction began in December 1935.

First, using local workmen, Pottsville sandstone was dug by hand from a quarry just a few hundred yards away from the site. It was then taken away in an old delivery truck the Kaufmanns sent from Pittsburgh and by horse-drawn sleds. This stone was to be used for all the load-bearing pillars and walls, whereas reinforced concrete, one of the exciting new materials that were invented in the latter half of the nineteenth century, was going to be used for the cantilevered levels. Trees and vegetation were cleared, but only as strictly necessary, and April 1936 saw the first sample wall being built

and foundation lines marked. The foundation piers and retaining walls followed. In August concrete was poured for the first-floor overhang, and the second-floor slab was finished by mid-September. The third floor was constructed in December, at which point the masonry was complete. Concerns about cracks in the concrete, causing Kaufmann to call in outside engineers, delayed work slightly, but by April 1937 the whole shell of the house was finished and work started on the interior. A few months later the house was complete, coming in way over budget at around $80,000. In December 1937 the family stayed at Fallingwater with houseguests for the first time and after the weekend stay wrote to Wright telling him they were absolutely delighted with it.

Throughout the construction the Kaufmanns took a keen interest in the building process and were often on site to see how things were progressing. Wright, too, made a number of visits.

A separate guesthouse, farther up the hill, was designed in 1938 and completed in 1939. It incorporated a four-car garage (Wright was a huge fan of the automobile, deeming it to be democratic) and servants' quarters. This added another $65,000 or so to the final bill-slightly more than half what the Kaufmanns paid for their house in town.

ABOVE: *Foundation level. The old bridge over Bear Run was removed and the new bridge started in April 1936 at the same time as Wright made his second site visit.*

RIGHT: *The ground floor roof level. Frank Lloyd Wright's design devotes almost as much floor space to the outdoor terraces as for the indoor rooms.*

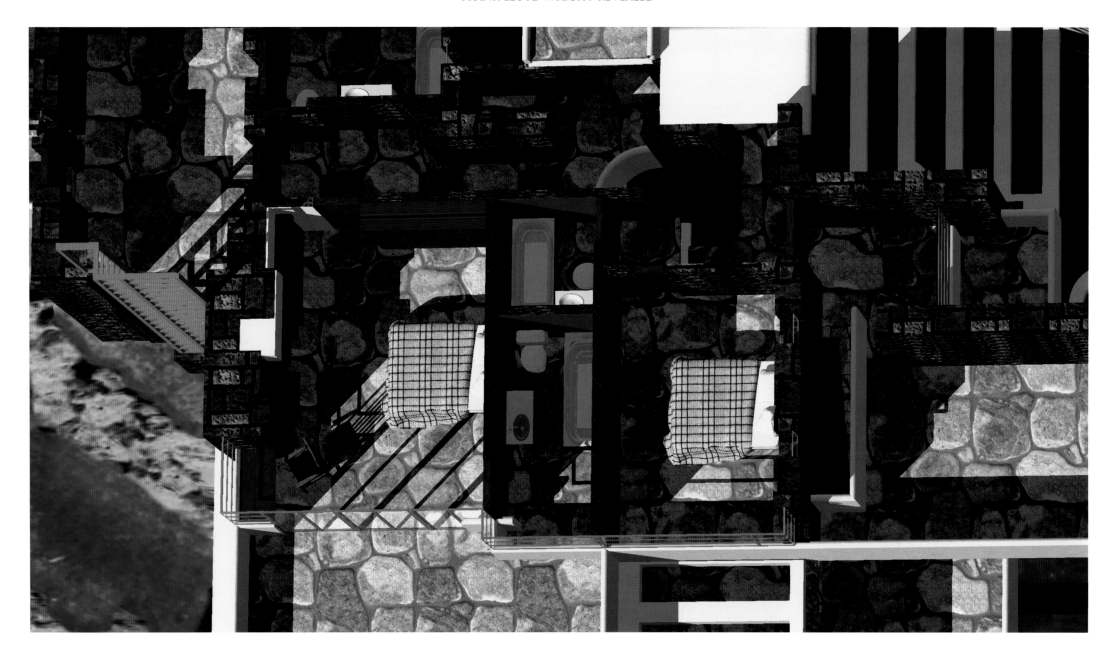

ABOVE: *The first floor roof. A 1991 poll of members of the American Institute of Architects voted Fallingwater "the best all-time work of American architecture."*

THE HOUSE DESCRIBED

Fallingwater is set on the north side of the stream, nestling into the south-facing hillside. Its three low main levels stack back up over the waterfall like natural rock ledges, with other terraces and ledges interlocking at right angles to each other. To one side the stone tower with its column of windows, housing the kitchen and the two bedrooms on top of one another, forms a solid core to the house, carrying the main pipes and wiring, and counterbalancing the cantilevered terraces.

The lowest "tray" is the main floor of the house, functioning as a living, dining, and reception area without divisions between them. From it there are views in three directions, with terraces leading out on two sides-one facing upstream, the other overhanging the rocks and water. Above, the middle level's large terrace forms the roof of the living room; here are the two main bedrooms. Each of these rooms also has its own terrace. The top level of the house, smaller still, contains a study and tiny bedroom, both with access to yet another terrace.

Characterizing the exterior are the steel window frames painted in Cherokee red, a favorite color of Wright's (even his car was that color), the rough, layered effect of the stonework to imitate the natural sandstone in the gorge, and the pale, smoothed surfaces of the concrete

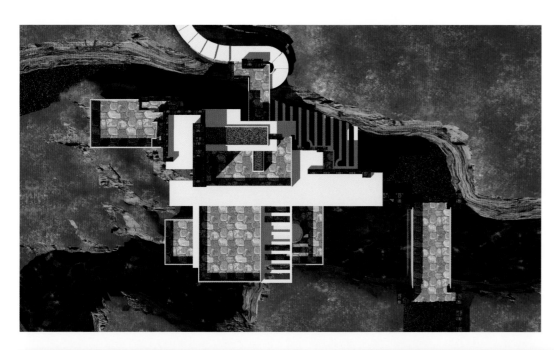

LEFT: *Plan view. The Laurel Highlands region of western Pennsylvania through which the Bear Run stream flows was once the home of Monongahela Indian settlements, and later the hunting grounds of the Iroquois.*

BELOW: *The first floor terrace. When the first floor cantilever was poured additional steel was added to strengthen the concrete without Wright's knowledge or approval.*

NEXT SPREAD: *The waterfall on Bear Run is stunningly set in a beautiful spot and was a Kaufmann family favorite even before the building of their house. Mr Kaufmann in particular loved to listen to the sound of the rushing waters.*

layers painted an apricot color. Wright's initial idea had been to use gold leaf on the concrete, to emulate the color of dying rhododendron leaves, but Kaufmann considered this to be too extravagant and dissuaded him.

The entrance to the house does not reveal itself readily (as is so often the case with Wright's houses) and is reached by crossing a twenty-eight-foot-long bridge straddling the stream on the east side of the building. There is then a walk of about sixty feet along part of the driveway, where straight concrete beams form an overhead trellis. Once found, tucked away by a little square pool, the door leads into a small foyer, which in turn leads into the

spectacular main living area.

Practically the whole of the outer walls of this huge, much-photographed room are glass, with doors opening onto the terrace jutting out over the waterfall, and views of the trees on the opposite bank. The edge of the terrace is turned up to produce a rounded parapet. Steep, suspended stone steps lead down from a sliding glass hatchway inside the living room to a small platform and plunge-pool in the middle of the stream beneath the east terrace. The bronze statue placed here by Wright is Mother and Child (1949) by Lithuanian-born French sculptor Jaques Lipchitz (1891-1973). Although the steps were expensive and served no real useful purpose, Wright insisted that they were essential to the ethos of the house.

A broad band of casement windows runs round the walls of the Great Room, as it is often known, with no upright glazing bar at the corners. When the windows are opened the corners disappear-this one of Wright's signature devices and can be seen in many of his houses. His idea of "window walls" was to bring the outside in, and vice versa, to increase the sense of spaciousness and expand the horizons. Window drapes were thought to be unnecessary, breaking the continuity between inside and outside. The relatively low ceilings of the room (barely six-and-a-half feet) give it a safe, protective feeling, drawing your eye to the outside. The floor-like those in the rest of the house-is stone, cut from the same nearby quarry as the walls and thus echoing the surrounding natural rocky terrain. Wright stipulated that the floor slabs be highly waxed so they would look wet, as if at the bottom of a stream. Nor is the floor entirely even, and in the interests of stability Mrs. Kaufmann preferred to use the three-legged dining chairs she brought from Italy, rather than the barrel chairs Wright designed to go around the table.

Built-in bookcases and long, low seats (all designed by Wright) seem to grow from the walls of the Great Room to eliminate clutter, and a huge fireplace dominates the

LEFT: *Fallingwater is the only Wright house open to the public that still contains its original furnishings and art works.*

ABOVE: *Low ceilings throughout the house provide a feeling of shelter and security as well as leading the eye out to the wooded valley beyond.*

back wall from floor to ceiling. In front of the fireplace boulders from the hill-reported to be Mr. Kaufmann's favorite sunbathing and picnic spot before Fallingwater was built-break through the floor. Instead of being cut back flush with the waxed floor, the boulders are raised and left unpolished, so as to resemble rocks emerging naturally from a stream.

Next to the fire an eighteen-gallon, red, cast-iron spherical wine-warmer sits in a specially carved semicircular niche. Wright suspended it on a pivot so that it could be swung out over the fire when guests arrived and they could be offered a welcome drink.

Soft furnishings are in natural, earthy

hues, with no busy, distracting patterns or designs, but here and there are bright accents of yellow and orange, so there is nothing dull about the overall effect. Curved shelves jut out from the stonework with no visible means of support, like fungi growing from a tree trunk.

Between the fireplace and dining table is the door to the kitchen, a smallish, utilitarian room almost entirely enclosed by the stone walls hugging the hillside, with windows looking out to the terrace suspended above the falls. The steel cabinets chosen by the Kaufmanns, the red linoleum floor, and the AGA cooker all remain.

Opposite the kitchen door, stairs lead

ABOVE: *West terrace. Work started here in November 1936. The cement for the terrace was mixed in a single cement-mixer then wheelbarrowed into position and poured out. The parapets were formed by hand using a shovel. As the cement set it was smoothed down and the joints trowelled over with a thin mix of cement.*

RIGHT: *The stone used for Fallingwater was quarried on the estate and is called Pottsville sandstone. It is a light gray conglomerate of gray to white sandstone with thin coal seams and minor shale horizons (cyclothems).*

LEFT: *View of the bedroom and bathroom and long feature window. All the non-structural wood used in the house is North Carolina black walnut—Juglans nigra—a rare and much sought after native hardwood prized for its hard, fine, straight grained qualities.*

ABOVE: *The west terrace. This had to be removed and recast following the discovery of new fractures in the south parapet wall over the center bolster beam.*

up between stone walls to the second-floor hall and the master bedroom, known as Mrs. Kaufmann's room. From this room, too, glass doors lead out onto the terrace, which on this level is much larger than the room itself and has uninterrupted views in three directions. Inside the bedroom another striking stone fireplace, with projecting stone ledges, dominates. One wall is covered in horizontally placed wood veneer. The smaller bedroom used by Mr. Kaufmann, on this level, is above the kitchen, so it also sits snugly at the back of the house. His desk is built into the wall by the window. At the back, up a few steps, a long terrace projects to the west of the house. On the third floor, a bit like a secret aerie, a long gallery faces another terrace and the small bedroom and study used by Edgar Jr..

Throughout the house each door is made from a single piece of wood with minimal door frames and hinges that fold into the wood with the economy and precision associated with ships' interiors. Built-in wooden cupboards and shelves utilize every corner. Even the stairway is lined with bookcases.

The bathrooms are comfortable, with cork-lined walls and floors (fashionable in the 1930s for its warmth and noiselessness), built-in vanity units, and

and decorated just as the family left it. Among the items, numbering not far short of a thousand, are artworks by American ornithologist and bird artist John James Audubon (1785-1851), American goldsmith and jeweler Louis Comfort Tiffany (1848-1933), Mexican muralist Diego Rivera (1886-1957), Finnish architect and designer Alvar Aalto (1898-1976) and Pablo Picasso (1881-1973), plus six Japanese woodblock prints that had been gifts from Wright. Wright began collecting prints in 1905, when he first visited Japan, and went on to become a serious collector and dealer of Japanese art.

Chief among the collection, however, are the pieces of veneered black walnut furniture that Wright designed specifically for the house and had made by the Gillen Woodworking Company of Milwaukee. A particular feature of the furniture is that the wood grain runs horizontally rather than vertically: Wright particularly stipulated this to help prevent warping in the damp, riverside setting. Pieces include seating,

LEFT *The south west corner. The cantilevers mimic the natural pattern of the rock ledges and are reinforced concrete slabs that project from the rock to pull the house out over the stream.*

BELOW: *The north west corner. Wright placed the house over the falls in a series of cantilevered concrete "trays," anchored to masonry walls made of the same Pottsville sandstone as the rock ledges.*

bookshelves, tables of varying sizes, a dining-room table, desks, chairs, and lamps.

Everywhere in the house the sound of the falling water is omnipresent. As Wright said, "You listen to the sound of water as you listen to the quiet of the country."

TODAY

Edgar Kaufmann Jr. donated the house to the Western Pennsylvania Conservancy (which had been established in 1932) in 1963 after inheriting the property from his father in 1955 (his mother had died three years earlier). By then Edgar Jr. was a curator of the Museum of Modern Art in New York, but he continued to use the house as a holiday home. It had been Edgar Sr.'s wish that the property, together with several hundred acres of land, should eventually be entrusted to the conservancy. Edgar Jr. played a key role in the administration of the house and land after the handover and often visited the house after tours to the public began in 1964, until his death in 1989. The house is a National Historic Landmark, one of the nationally significant historic places designated by the secretary of the interior. Criteria include possessing exceptional value or quality in illustrating or interpreting the heritage of the United States.

Preservation of Fallingwater has always been of key concern, first by the

ABOVE: *First and second floor terrace. Relations between architect and client became strained as the building progressed with each claiming that the other was going behind their back on decision-making.*

RIGHT: *Second floor terrace. Cracks appeared in the parapets and terraces even while the building was under construction.*

PAGE 102 AND 103: *Top floor roof. By the 1980s Fallingwater had fallen into a poor state of condition and thorough and expensive restoration and renovation was undertaken to save the building from decay and collapse.*

Kaufmann family, who monitored the cracks and movement in the terraces that appeared early on, then by the Western Pennsylvania Conservancy. Since the conservancy's ownership there has been an ongoing program of restoration. Waterproofing of roofs and terraces has been carried out; the original single-pane glass has been replaced with ultraviolet-filtering glass; rubberized membranes have been placed under some of the flagstone flooring; the outside has been painted with cement-based paint; a sewage treatment unit has been installed; steps are continually been taken to preserve the woodwork; and the house has been rewired.

One of the major concerns (as has been the case since the house was first built) is the instability of the cantilevers and in the 1990s it became apparent that the house would fall into the water without drastic remedial action. As a result the main terrace on the first level was structurally strengthened and three of the four main beams, as well as several of the smaller cross joists, were post-tensioned, lifting the cantilevers by five inches. The work was completed in time for the house to be reopened in 2002. There has also been some re-landscaping of the plot, with new pathways and parking areas to accommodate the increasing number of visitors.

ABOVE: *Detail of the south-east corner terrace. The building was deliberately designed to blur the normal distinctions between the "inside" and the "outside" so that the spaces flow into and through each other to create a seamless experience. Frank Lloyd Wright was hugely influential with this concept of open plan living.*

TOP RIGHT: *View of the footbridge. The living room, master bedroom terrace, and Edgar Kaufmann, Sr.'s terrace cantilevers all suffered problems with sagging and cracking right from the start and Edgar Kaufmann engaged engineers to make annual surveys from 1941 to 1955 to assess the ongoing structural problems.*

BOTTOM RIGHT: *The road bridge. A 1994 structural survey of Fallingwater put the building's problems down to mistakes in the design and detailing of the reinforcement, particularly of the cantilevers. Accordingly an extensive renovation program was started.*

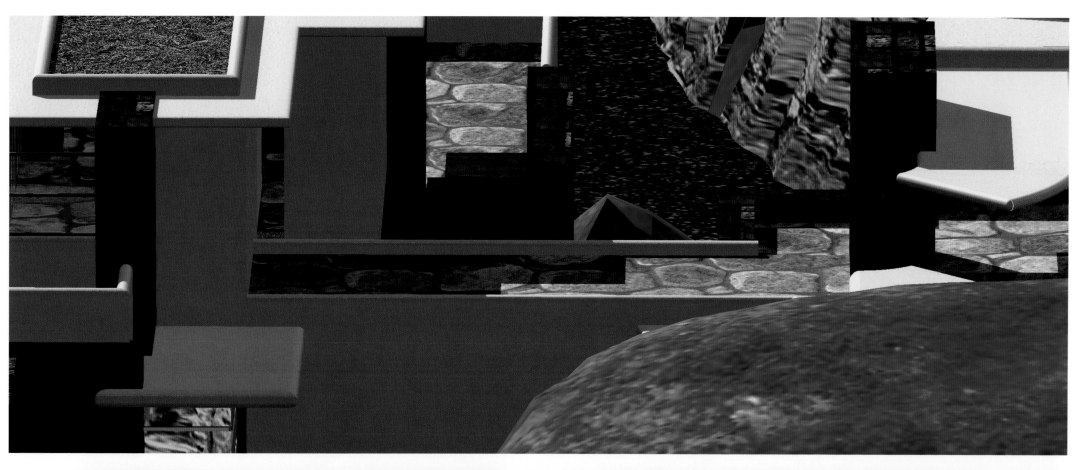

LEFT: *The south east corner. The building is orientated to the south east—as Wright personally preferred—with the floors extending in horizontal bands out over the waterfall.*

ABOVE: *Frank Lloyd Wright first saw the site at Bear Run in December 1934 and he was immediately struck by the beauty of the area and the music of the stream.*

PREVIOUS PAGE: *The river steps lead directly from the living room to the stream to deliberately tie the building in even more firmly with its surroundings.*

LEFT: *The view from downstream. The house rises 30 feet above the rushing mountain stream known as Bear Run, which is as integral to the building as any of its other elements.*

BELOW: *Between 1995 and 1998 the entire exterior was chemically stripped of its previous 14 or so layers of paint, then patched and repainted with a specially formulated coating system that allows the building to "breathe," while at the same time repelling moisture.*

To do this work, at a cost of several million dollars, the conservancy was given a grant from the Commonwealth of Pennsylvania through the Redevelopment Assistance Capital Program (RACP), as well as receiving funds from several other sources.

The Western Pennsylvania Conservancy takes great care to remain true to Wright's ethos concerning the house's relationship with its surroundings, and no design alterations are made in the name of restoration. However the use of new technology and materials has been necessary to maintain the structural integrity of the house, as Fallingwater's long-term preservation is of paramount importance.

CHAPTER IV

THE JACOBS
SECOND RESIDENCE

THE JACOBS SECOND RESIDENCE

ABOVE: *The house is approached on the east side via a tunnel that pierces the berm and opens out onto the terrace, overlooking the garden. Wright was looking at an organic design to create an organic home when he got this commission. This residence was devised to respond exactly to the Jacobs' needs as well as to their budget and the site location. Rather to Wright's frustration, such a very personal collaboration and prevailing circumstances made the building near impossible to adapt for future clients. This is why the building remains unique.*

HISTORY

Herbert Jacobs and his wife, Katherine, were one of the few clients lucky enough to have two houses built for them by Wright, and both of them were "firsts." This, the second, was the prototype for a series of curved plans that Wright termed solar hemicycle houses (semicircular houses facing the sun). It is located in what is now the Madison, Wisconsin, suburb of Middleton.

Several years earlier, in 1937, Wright had built the Jacobs a modest house (then called Westmoreland) in Madison, Wisconsin. Herb Jacobs, a young journalist with a wife and small daughter working as a reporter on the Capital Times, had been introduced to Wright through his wife's cousin, Clarence Westcott, who knew Wright through his time as a student at Taliesin. The couple had limited funds at their disposal and challenged Wright to build them a house within a budget of $5,000. Wright was keen to take up the gauntlet because it was exactly in line with his long-held dream of "democratic" architecture and his commitment to building houses of individual design and artistic merit that were affordable to the average American family. The finished house, consisting of about fifteen hundred square feet, came in at $5,500, a figure that included Wright's fee of $450. It was the one and only time in Wright's career that he guaranteed a client a pre-agreed budget.

This commission was the first of his Usonian houses to be built (it is sometimes referred to as Usonian Number One), although there had been previous plans for others that were never executed. Like most of the houses that followed, this one was based on a rectangular grid to simplify the building process. To keep costs down it had one story, a flat roof, and no foundation. The concrete slab that formed the base contained heating coils, placed on a bed of sand so the warmth of the earth would naturally warm the house. The walls of the house were made up of three layers of laminated board, screwed together and without conventional stud framing, which were held up by masonry pillars. Bookcases lined the interior walls to help strengthen them and to reduce clutter.

L-shaped and with its back turned to the street, the house afforded the occupants privacy to the outside world, but on its private side opened up with full height expanses of window to a large garden. Occupying one arm inside was the large open living space and the kitchen, with the bedrooms in the other wing. Where the two arms of the building met was the fireplace, forming the masonry core to the house that also housed the utilities, so that pipe runs were as short as possible. Wright also invented the carport at this time, claiming that cars didn't need to be kept in more costly garages. Happy

ABOVE: *Frank Lloyd Wright was in his seventies when he designed the Jacobs Second Residence. During this period he was experimenting with the idea of using designs based on the helix and a collection of circles; nobody else was working with these concepts at the time. The solar aspects of the building were pioneering—the berm to deflect wind, alongside the two story wall of south facing glass.*

TOP LEFT: *West elevation. In early 1944 Wright showed the Jacobs the design he had come up with—it was his first solar hemicycle and has been described as a pioneer of passive solar design.*

BOTTOM LEFT: *North elevation. The back of the house—the northern elevation—is half buried within the hill and protected from the cold winter north-west wind by a berm rising nearly to the top of the wall. This also encourages the warm southern winds to lift over the house.*

RIGHT: *South-east elevation. Wright first saw the site in July 1943 when he chose the precise location for the new house. Due to wartime restrictions on material and labor construction, the house was not started until 1946 when the war was over. It was completed in 1949.*

BELOW: *South elevation. The south façade makes the most of the winter sunshine by capturing every bit of available light with the use of an extensive ribbon of windows and glazed doors. This augments the warmth already provided by the gravity heat inside the floor.*

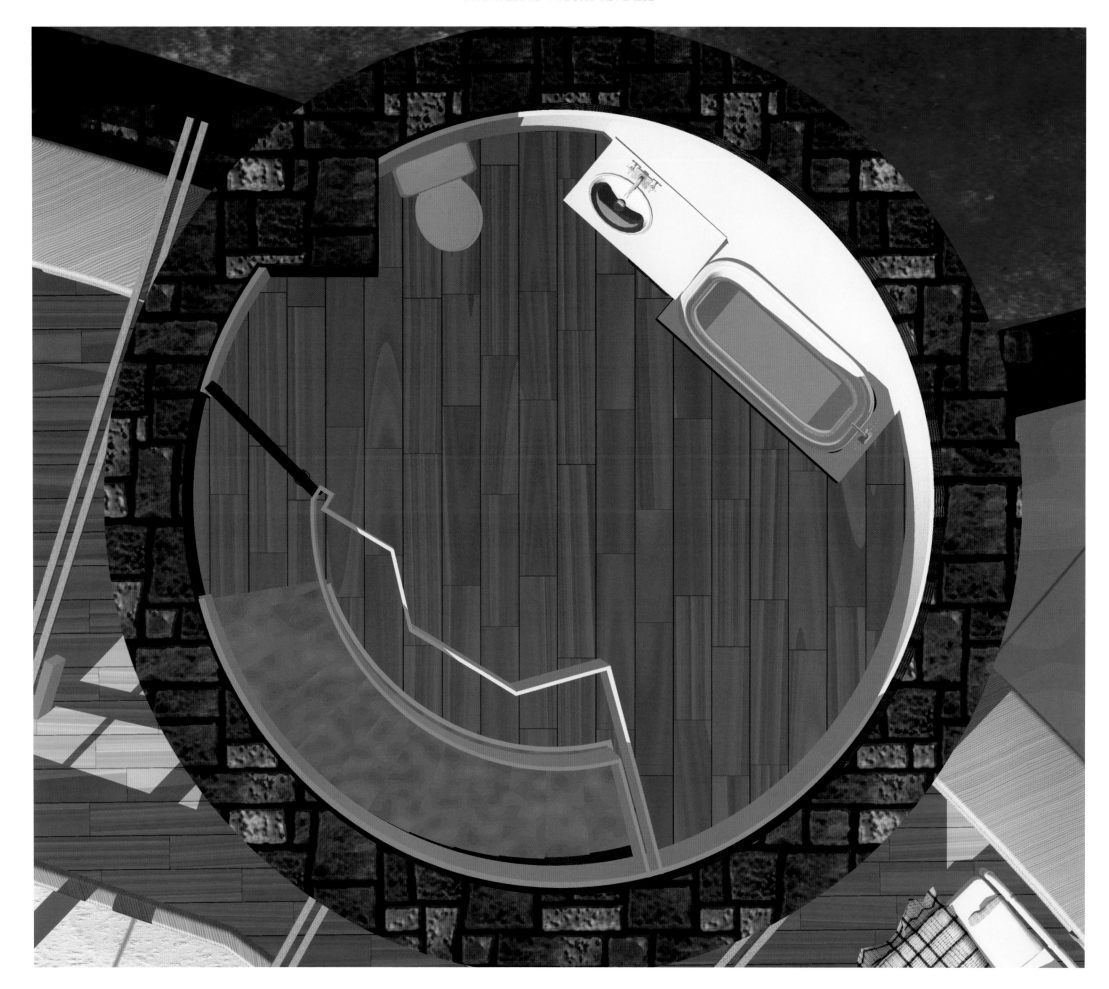

LEFT: *The bathroom is on the second floor of the tower which is located on the south side of the building and is partly within the main part of the house and partially in the berm. The tower also contains the staircase as well as the laundry and furnace on the first floor.*

BELOW: *The Jacobs Second Residence has been described as being the first truly Usonian house thanks to its concrete slab floor with underfloor heating and wood sandwich-wall construction which eliminated the need for conventional studs. Usonian was Wright's acronym for the United States of North America. The few walls within the house—really only in the bedrooms—are made of overlapping boards screwed to each other at their edges and set at a 30-degree angle relative to the floor.*

as the Jacobs were with this house, the family soon outgrew it and in 1942, wanting to move farther out into the countryside, bought a fifty-two-acre farm in what was then open prairie land nine miles from downtown Madison. Their intention from the start was to build another house there, with Wright as the architect, and discussions began in 1943. However the first design that Wright came up with was too lavish for Jacobs, so Wright returned to the drawing board.

By this time Wright was well into his seventies, but his career had gained a new momentum with the completion of the acclaimed Fallingwater and Johnson Wax Building under his belt. Despite the interruption of World War II, he designed

many houses that were completed later in the 1940s.

It was at this stage of his life that Wright began incorporating circles and spirals into his designs. He had always been fascinated by the symbolism of the circle, representing infinity, continuity, and the order of the cosmos, and had used it in his art-glass designs and murals, but previously his floor plans had been confined to rectilinear shapes. Now he was using its properties as a mathematical concept. One of the most spectacular examples of this addition to his repertoire is the Guggenheim Museum (completed in 1959, a few months after Wright's death) in New York, which he was commissioned to design in 1943. Round towers, porthole

windows, and circular skylights appeared in his buildings too.

Material shortages during World War II delayed construction of the Jacobs' second house until 1946 and because the family built most of the house themselves (as indeed they had their first house, to keep costs down), with some help from local workmen whom they contracted themselves, it wasn't finished until 1949. The cost was about $20,000.

THE HOUSE DESCRIBED

Wright's solar hemicycle houses, as he named them, took the energy-efficient concepts applied to his Usonian houses a stage further. With one wall curved against the northern aspect, and designed to make

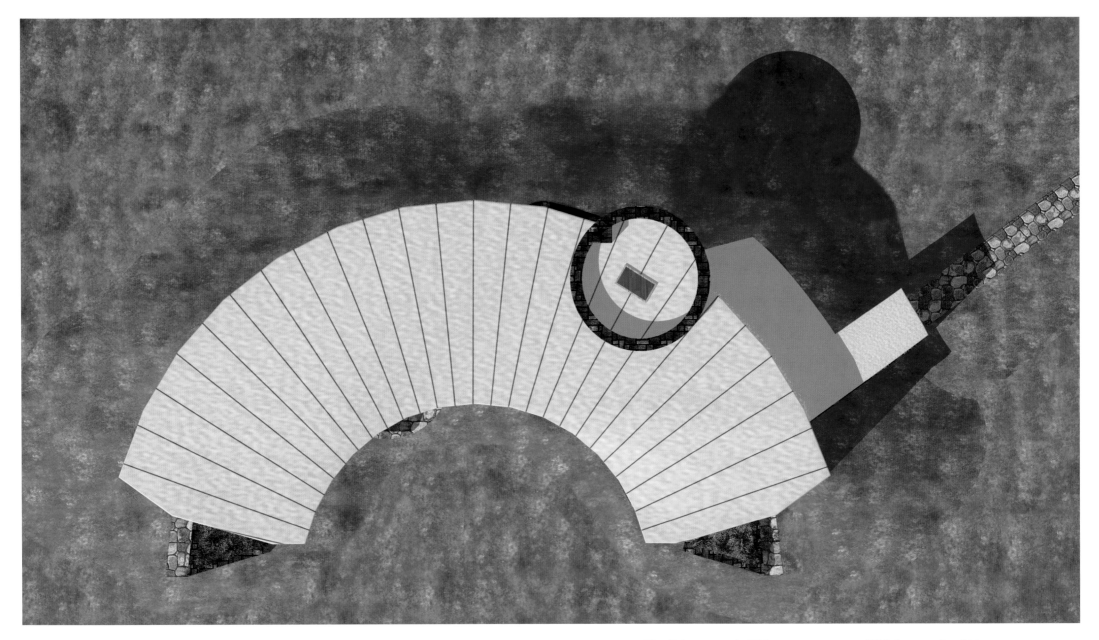

as much use of the sun and the earth as possible to heat the house in winter, they were in the vanguard of solar passive houses. The Jacobs House was also the first of a series of buildings that Wright built using plans of circles and semicircles.

The house is partially buried in the ground. It consists principally of a two-story semicircle, the curved front of which, composed almost entirely of glass to make maximum use of the sun's rays, is orientated to face south, while earth (the berm) is piled up against the solid rock northern wall to provide insulation and deflect the prevailing winds up and over the house. Aside from aesthetic considerations, the curved wall had the

advantage from an engineering point of view of being better able to withstand pressure-in this case from the berm, but the principle is often demonstrated in dams-than a straight wall.

When viewed from the northern side, all that emerges above what seems to be a grassy hill is the top of the round utility tower, about fifteen feet in diameter, that sits off-center astride the back wall of the house, and a strip of the slightly lower semicircular back wall inset with its narrow windows.

The way into the house is through a square, rock-lined passageway carved through the artificial hill, which leads to the sunken, open-air, circular garden. (The

PREVIOUS PAGE: *The living room is 17 feet wide by 80 feet long and in summer the wide overhanging eaves shield the living areas from the fierce sunshine. The glass frontage runs in a rhythm of one door, pair of doors, fixed glass pane, pair of doors, fixed glass pane, pair of doors, one door.*

ABOVE: *Wright conceived his new commission as an economic solar project that would be cost effective yet spare nothing in terms of the use of local stone, wood, concrete, and a little metal where necessary.*

excavated earth was used for the berm.) Forming the boundary of one half of this circle is the double-height glass wall of the semicircular house.

Inside, on the west side of the tower, the whole of the narrow (seventeen feet in depth), curved, ground-level space is taken up with the open living and dining area. A particular striking feature toward the western end of this room is the semicircle sunk eighteen inches into the floor that forms one half of a circular pool (complete with water and plants), with the deeper other half of the pool cutting into the edge of the garden on the other side of the glass wall. As well as being a highly decorative feature, the pond, by narrowing the width

of the room, serves to create a slightly secluded area at that end of the space, which has been variously used over the years as a study or quiet area, or for watching television. Set into the curved stone outer wall of the tower is the fireplace, with a simple wooden shelf embedded in the stone serving as a mantelpiece. A step in the back wall step creates a shelf, running round the length of the room.

At this level a passage leads around the front of tower to the remainder of the semicircle, which is occupied by the kitchen, about fourteen feet in width. The tower itself contains the staircase, which rises up the curving inner south wall to the

ABOVE: *First floor plan. The house consists of a series of circles or semi circles. The main area is a two story semi-circle segment of about 120 degrees, alongside a few circular rooms such as the utility tower, bathroom, garden, and plunge pool. Wright wanted his buildings to flow and get away from the use of the right angle. Even the fireplace is semicircular.*

upper level. It also houses a large bathroom on the second level and a utility room at ground level. To the east is the master bedroom, located above the kitchen. There are skylights above the stairwell and in the bathroom.

In a system not unlike the one used at Wright's Oak Park studio, the whole of the second floor is cantilevered from the back wall and suspended by steel rods, which in turn are suspended from narrow strips of board running from the back masonry wall to the window wall across the roof. This creates a sort of platform, giving the living area and kitchen a partial ceiling with a height of about 6 feet 4 inches to the rafters. Upstairs the ceilings are a few inches higher. The front of the balcony, bounded by a three-foot-high wooden parapet, falls short of the window wall by just under four feet, allowing heat to rise up from the downstairs and unifying the two spaces.

Over the years, and with its different owners, the main upper floor area above the living area has been adapted to suit different requirements. When it was built the whole space was completely open, but the Jacobs divided it into four bedrooms for their children. Later it became two bedrooms separated by a living area. Along the back wall of the house, allowing light into the balcony rooms and the main bedroom, are small windows-little more than two feet high-which are hinged to open inward. A vertical window in the northwest corner of the west bedroom descends into the same corner of the living room below.

LEFT: *The Jacobs family themselves, especially Herbert Jacobs, did much of the construction work with only minimal help from local workmen. To save money they used their own farm workers as stonemasons when they were not busy on the farm. They made remarkably few changes to Wright's plan drawings. He approved so much of the build that he brought prospective clients to view the result.*

Outside, the five-foot roof overhang (nearly double this though at each end of the semicircle) to the front is precisely calculated to shade the interior from the fierce, high sun of summer, ensuring that the concrete base to the house and stone back wall remain cool, while in winter the lower arc of the sun's path means the converse is true, allowing the masonry to warm up by day and radiate heat into the house at night.

To echo the limestone outcrops in the area, the double stone walls, about three feet thick, were laid in horizontal courses that alternately projected and receded and all the joints were deeply scored-apparently by Katherine Jacobs.

Unlike his first Jacobs house, which was placed on a slab of concrete set into gravel, Wright built foundations for the heavier stone walls here. Dug by hand by Jacobs himself, they were five feet deep and filled with crushed rock to allow any water to drain away without freezing. The concrete slab then rested on top. The flat roof of the house slopes slightly down to the north, allowing water to drip into the berm.

The separate, flat-roofed barn and carport was built by Herb Jacobs and was not part of Wright's plan. It was constructed from cement blocks and then plastered over in an attempt to blend it with the house.

TODAY

The Jacobs Second Residence has always been in private ownership and remains so today. This means that it is not open to the public, although it was designated a National Historic Landmark in July 2003. Unfortunately, since it was built, building has encroached on the surrounding open prairie and it is now a part of the suburban development of Middleton.

Dr. John Moore, professor of chemistry at the University of Wisconsin-Madison, and his wife, Elizabeth, who also works in the department of chemistry, moved into the house in July 1989 and live

there today. Prior to that the Taylor family owned the house.

In 1962, when Herb Jacobs left his reporting job and moved his family to California to teach at the University of California-Berkeley, the house was sold to Mr. William Taylor; Taylor was taking up a post as a history professor at the University of Wisconsin-Madison. He and his wife had five children, ranging in age from ten to nineteen, so to create more space the barn that had been used by Katherine Jacobs as an art studio was converted into a separate room for the two older boys. Plumbing, door, and windows were added to make it habitable.

In 1968 the Taylors divorced and starting in 1969 the house was rented out during the school year to university students, with Mrs. Taylor and any of her children who were around moving back in during the summer vacations. This

arrangement continued until around 1976, when Mrs. Taylor returned to the house permanently and lived there with one of her sons, Bill, and friends from the university.

During this unsettled period in the early 1970s the fabric of the house seriously deteriorated due to lack of funds and a succession of sometimes careless tenants. The cost of heating the house in winter alone was staggering (the heating bill in one year had been known to reach $3,500), so in 1980 a new boiler was installed, in the hope that it would be more efficient and cost effective. Unfortunately, though, the underfloor pipes were damaged and the house was vacated shortly afterward.

Later, in 1983, Bill bought the house from his mother and returned to start restoring it, a mammoth and costly task as years of neglect and inherent building

problems had taken their toll. With the aid of bank loans and help from his stepfather, Taylor engaged a contractor to tackle the exterior and construction work. Taylor himself undertook much of the interior work.

Renovations, both essential and to bring the house more in line with late twentieth-century living standards, included adding a new radiant floor heating system, installing a high-efficiency furnace and air-conditioning, replacing the roof, replacing the windows (originally taken from old store fronts) with triple-pane glass, replacing rotten woodwork, and updating the plumbing and wiring. Taylor also turned the four upstairs rooms above the living area into three rooms, put a skylight in the master bedroom and turned the indoor half of the circular pool into a whirlpool.

ABOVE: *The flat roof is sloped to drain into the berm. On completion the house had cost the Jacobs something in the region of $15-20,000, a not inconsiderable sum for the period, especially when a lot of the labor was done by the Jacobs themselves.*

OPPOSITE PAGE: *Floor plans of the building. The bedrooms are on the upper level and to keep the space below entirely open and clear the second floor is hung from the roof with metal rods. The family swimming pool is located on the southern side of the house, half in and half outside.*

INFO

The Jacobs Second Residence has always been in private ownership and remains so today. It is not open to the public, although it was designated a National Historic Landmark in July 2003.

3995 Shawn Trail, Middleton, Wisconsin 53562

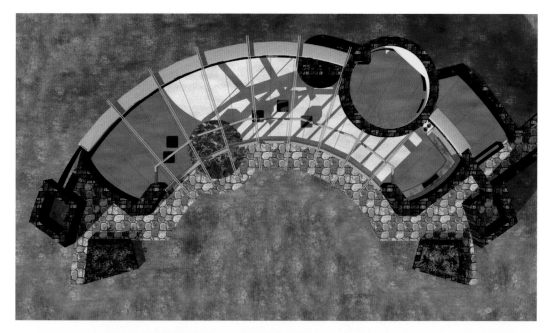

CHAPTER V

THE MARSHALL ERDMAN PREFAB HOUSES

THE MARSHALL ERDMAN PREFAB HOUSES

PREVIOUS PAGE: *Frank Iber Residence, Stevens Point, Wisconsin, 1956.*

ABOVE: *The prefabs all followed the same basic layout, they consisted of a masonry core (an "L" shape for #1) with the exterior made of textured and painted Masonite board (a pressed-wood product) decorated with horizontal battens. The interior was panelled with quarter inch thick mahogany plywood.*

RIGHT: *Frank Lloyd Wright believed that buildings should harmonize with their surroundings not sit in defiant conflict. To that end he endeavored to blend his buildings into the surrounding terrain through a combination of architectural line and use of local indigenous building materials. He called his ideal residence the "Natural House."*

HISTORY

Wright first met Marshall Erdman during the building of the Unitarian Meeting House in Wisconsin, a commission he accepted in 1947. He had connections with the Unitarian Society all his life and his parents were among the first members of the society. Erdman became the major contractor on the project. The church was on a low budget, and during construction Erdman got himself into personal debt to get the building finished. In 1952 Wright brought in the Taliesin Fellowship to finish off the interior detailing.

After the death of his mother when he was in his teens, Erdman-a Lithuanian, born Mausas Erdmanas in 1922-had been sent by his father to stay with his uncle in Chicago. Erdman knew no English, but went on to study architecture and engineering at the University of Illinois before joining the army in 1943. When the war was over he returned to education, this time studying political science at the University of Winsconsin. From there he went into the construction industry and in 1951, shortly after completing the Meeting House for Wright, Erdman founded Marshall Erdman & Associates with a dozen or so employees.

Wright had never lost his interest in the concept of mass-produced housing so when, in the mid-1950s, he came to hear about the prefabricated homes being produced by Erdman, Wright promptly claimed he could produce superior designs at half the cost. The two men collaborated on the project and Wright went on to design four types of prefab house in all, but only two, Prefab No 1 and Prefab No 2, were built.

Prior to building, Wright requested a site plan of the plot and photographs from his client, so he could then determine the best position for the house. The cost of the house included the major structural components, interior and exterior walls, floors, windows and doors, as well as cabinets and woodwork, but the client had to provide foundations, plumbing, heating units, electrical wiring, drywall, and paint.

PREFAB NO. 1

In the summer of 1956 the first of Wright's prefab plans was complete and by the fall construction work had begun on the prototype. This model house was built in 1956 on Anchorage Avenue in Madison, Wisconsin, and subsequently sold to Eugene Van Tamelen in 1957. Erdman eventually built eight other houses based on this model, three of which-the Jackson Residence, the Iber Residence, and the Mollica Residence-are also in Wisconsin. The Duncan Residence and the Post Residence are in Illinois, the Zaferiou Residence and the Cass Residence are in New York and the LaFond Residence is in Minnesota.

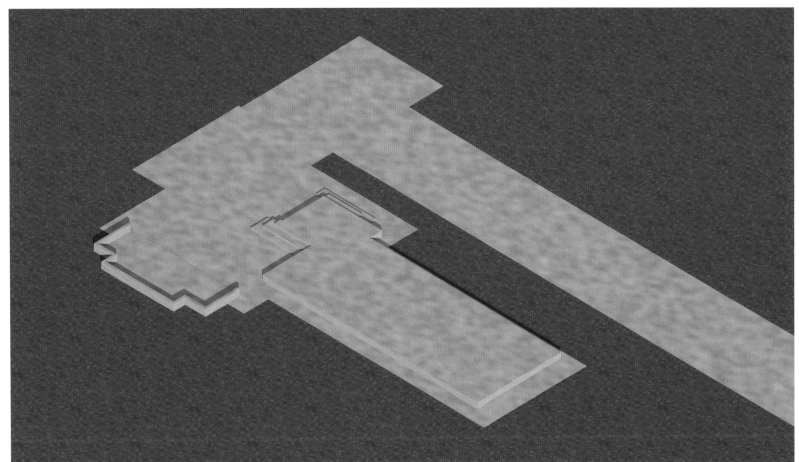

THIS PAGE: *Marshall Erdman had been the contractor for Wright's Unitarian Church and had finished the project off at his own expense. A few years later Wright heard that Erdman was attempting to produce mass market affordable housing—a pet project of his. Wright approached Erdman and announced that he could produce much better designs than the original architect. He believed that he could turn out a prefabricated house for $15,000, which was half as much as Erdman was charging for his own version. In fact they turned out to be much more expensive. Wright finalized his plans in spring 1956 and the first house Erdman and Wright produced was called the Erdman Prefab I and this was quickly sold to Eugene Van Tamelen in 1956. It is an L-shape with a masonry core and board and batten siding.*

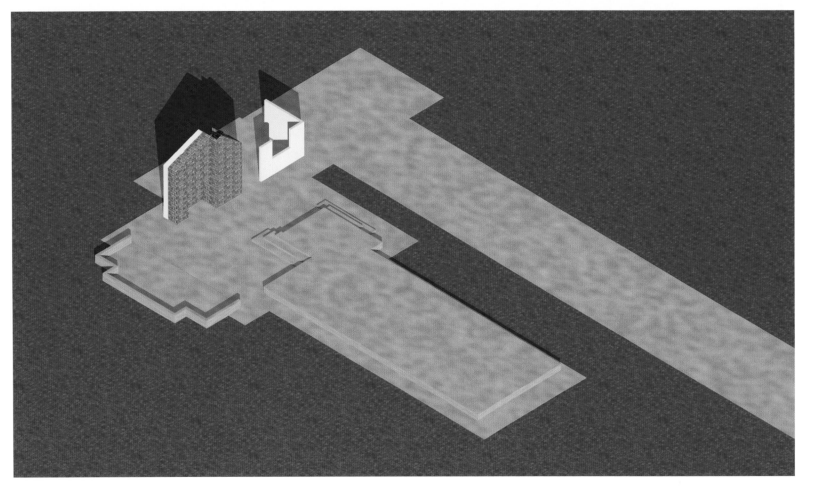

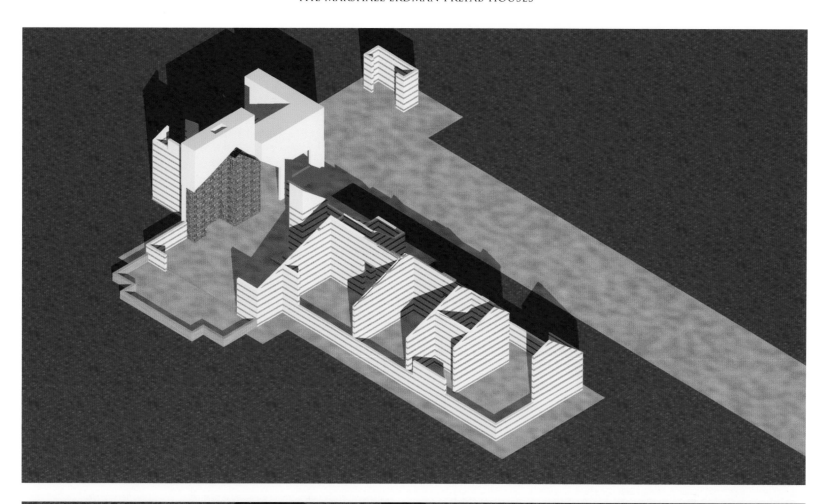

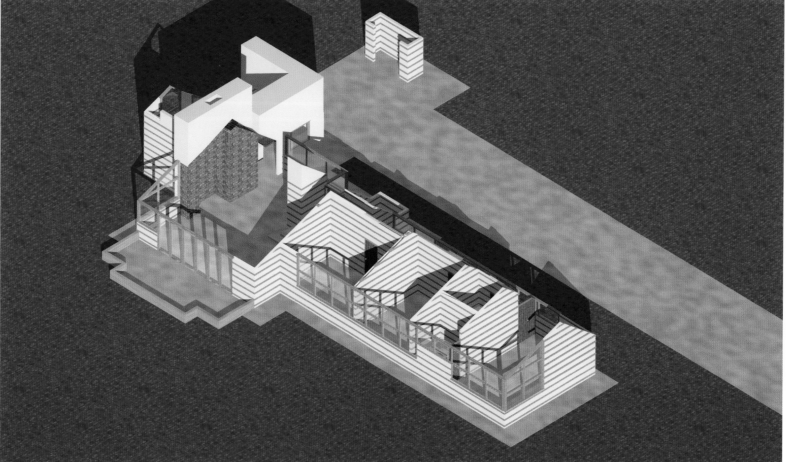

THIS PAGE: *Frank Lloyd Wright's prefabricated plans showed a single story house with a pitched-roofed bedroom wing joining a flat-roofed open plan living-cum-dining-cum-kitchen area that revolved around a large fireplace. Outside, a detached storage shed shared a flat roof with a carport. Clients liked the simplicity of the design but found the plan too small, so Wright was eventually prevailed upon to produce variations, which included a fourth bedroom and the possibility of a full or partial basement. The versions ranged in size between 1,860 to 2,400 square feet.*

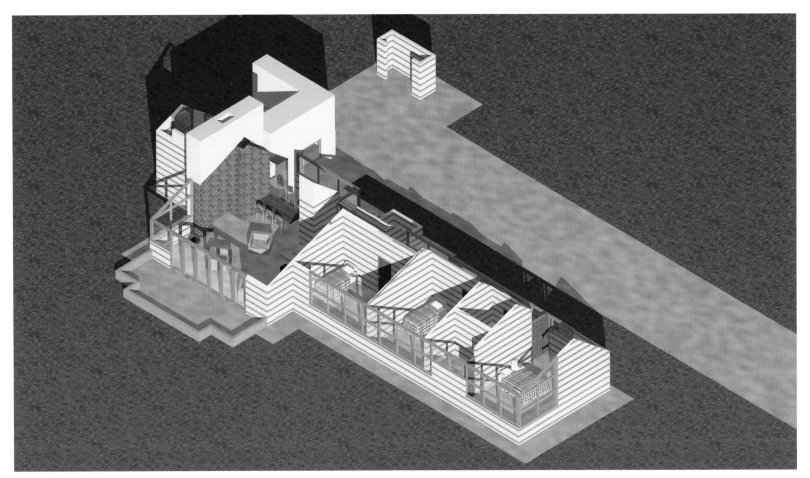

THIS PAGE: *Clients could choose some of the constituent elements depending on how much they wanted to spend, for example they were offered limestone, brick, or concrete block masonry or a combination of same; and for the roof either asphalt shingles held in place with battens or cedar shakes. The Van Tamelen Residence as the prototype building was much the most expensive of the prefabs to build. It is constructed of textile blocks and wood with wooden floors. The house was on the small side and the van Tamelen's later commissioned the Taliesin Associated Architects to greatly extend the living areas and dig out a full basement under their house.*

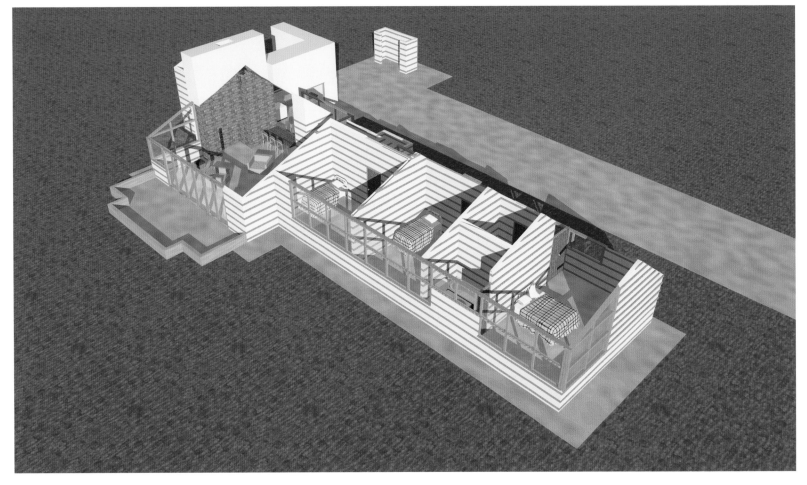

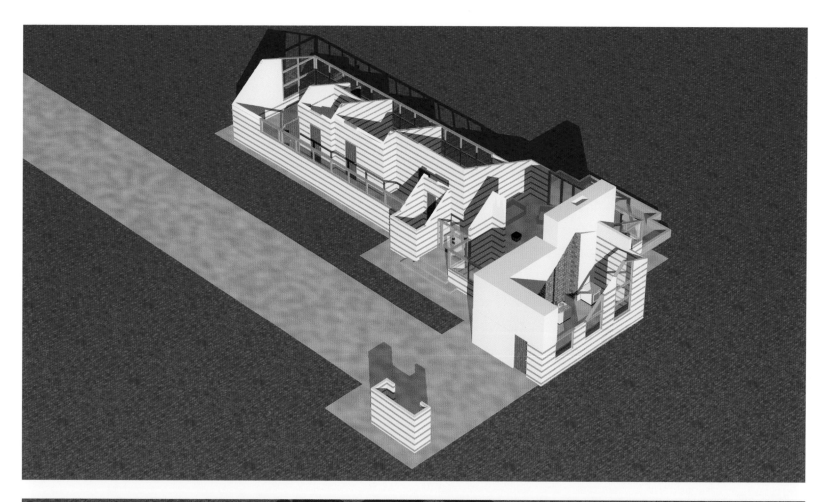

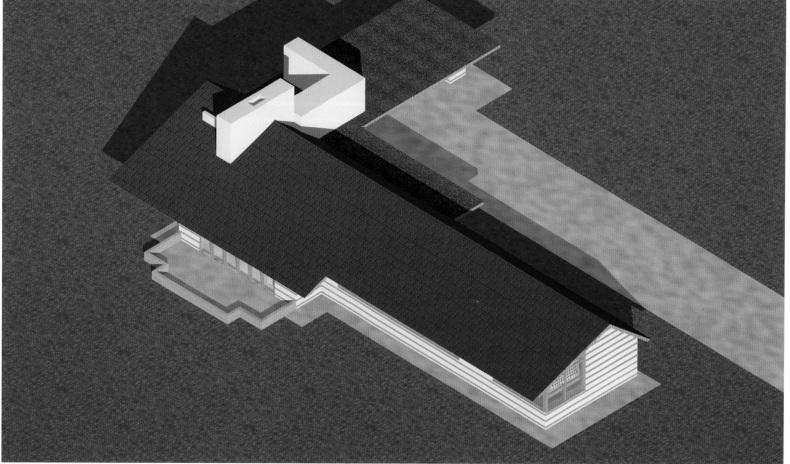

THIS PAGE: *When a client bought an Erdman prefab package he purchased all the major components (using standard builders trade sizes for economy) as well as cabinets and woodwork. Another cost cutting measure was achieved with the use of the ubiquitous standard Pella doors and Anderson windows. The buyer had to provide the site, the foundation, the plumbing fixtures, heating units, electric wiring, and drywall, plus the paint.*

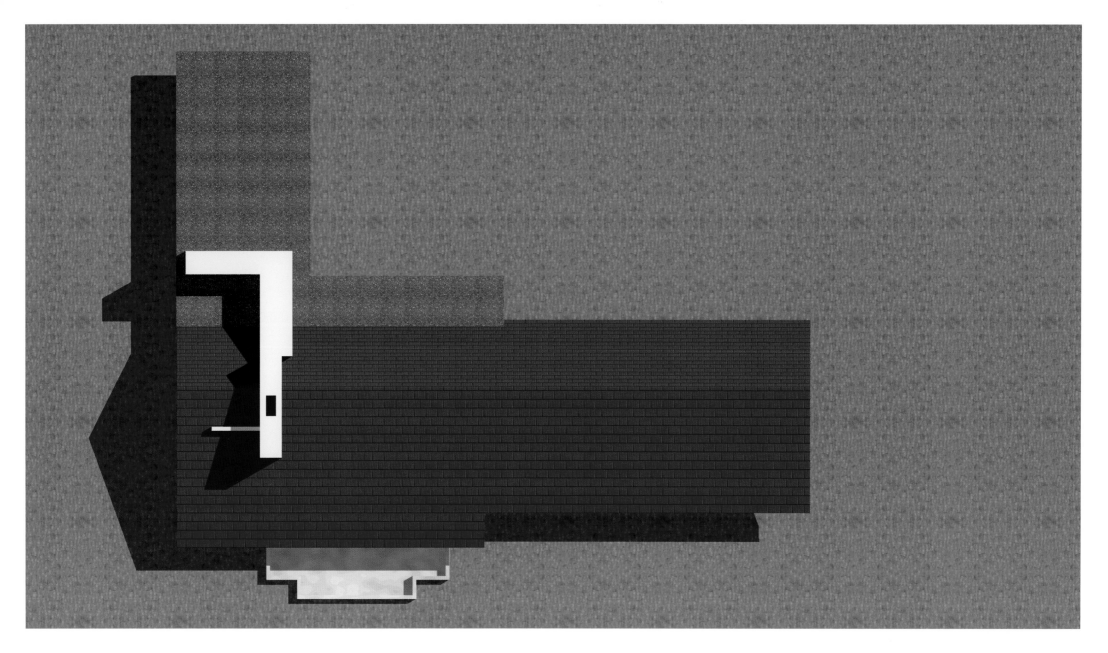

The Jackson Residence was the second house to be built. Dr Arnold and Lara Jackson had seen the Van Tamelen model and wanted their own version. One of their requirements was a garage. By this time Wright-who had invented the carport-despised the garage, but Dr Jackson claimed it was essential for him to be able to start his car on the coldest of mornings. Another variation was that their bedroom had extra windows, partly to let more sun into the room and partly to allow Mr. and Mrs. Jackson to be aware of the arrival of any visitors. There were three bedrooms in the house and a basement level with windows. In 1985 the house was moved from the Seminole Highway in Madison to Beaver Dam, Wisconsin, where a new foundation was built and extra structural support was added to the roof.

Next to be built was the Duncan Residence, for Elizabeth and Don Duncan. After visiting the two existing prefab houses, they requested the Jackson house model, but this was built with concrete blocks (rather than the more expensive limestone used for the Jackson house) and with a carport rather than a garage-again for cost reasons. The outside is painted the same color as the Van Tamelen Residence. The Iber Residnece was also built in 1957, for Frank Iber. This house has four bedrooms, a garage, and a basement with a long "window wall." No expense needed

LEFT: *The living room of the Frank Iber House. This was built in 1956 to the Marshall Erdman Prefab Design #1.*

ABOVE: *Even during construction Wright was notorious for quarreling with his clients if they wanted to make changes that he did not approve of—and would threaten to withdraw the sale of "his" building.*

NEXT SPREAD: *The Erdman prefabs were devised to provide affordable housing, but in practice they were too expensive and were bought instead by comfortably off professionals.*

LEFT AND ABOVE: *The Frank Iber House. The client had to provide Wright with photos of the site and a topographic map before he would approve the sale. He would then decide how the house would be positioned. He liked to make unannounced site visits— but ideally not talk to the clients. Upon completion Wright would visit the house and add his famous brick red tile with gold signature to the building if he approved of the work. This would be withheld until he was entirely satisfied.*

ABOVE: *Frank Iber House. Dr Iber bought his Prefab #1 in 1957. The house has limestone masonry and cedar shingles with contrasting (bleached) blond mahogany for fascia and soffits.*

RIGHT: *Although in his late eighties Frank Lloyd Wright was still thinking in original ways: in his lifetime he was able to see how his ideas influenced and inspired generations of architects and clients.*

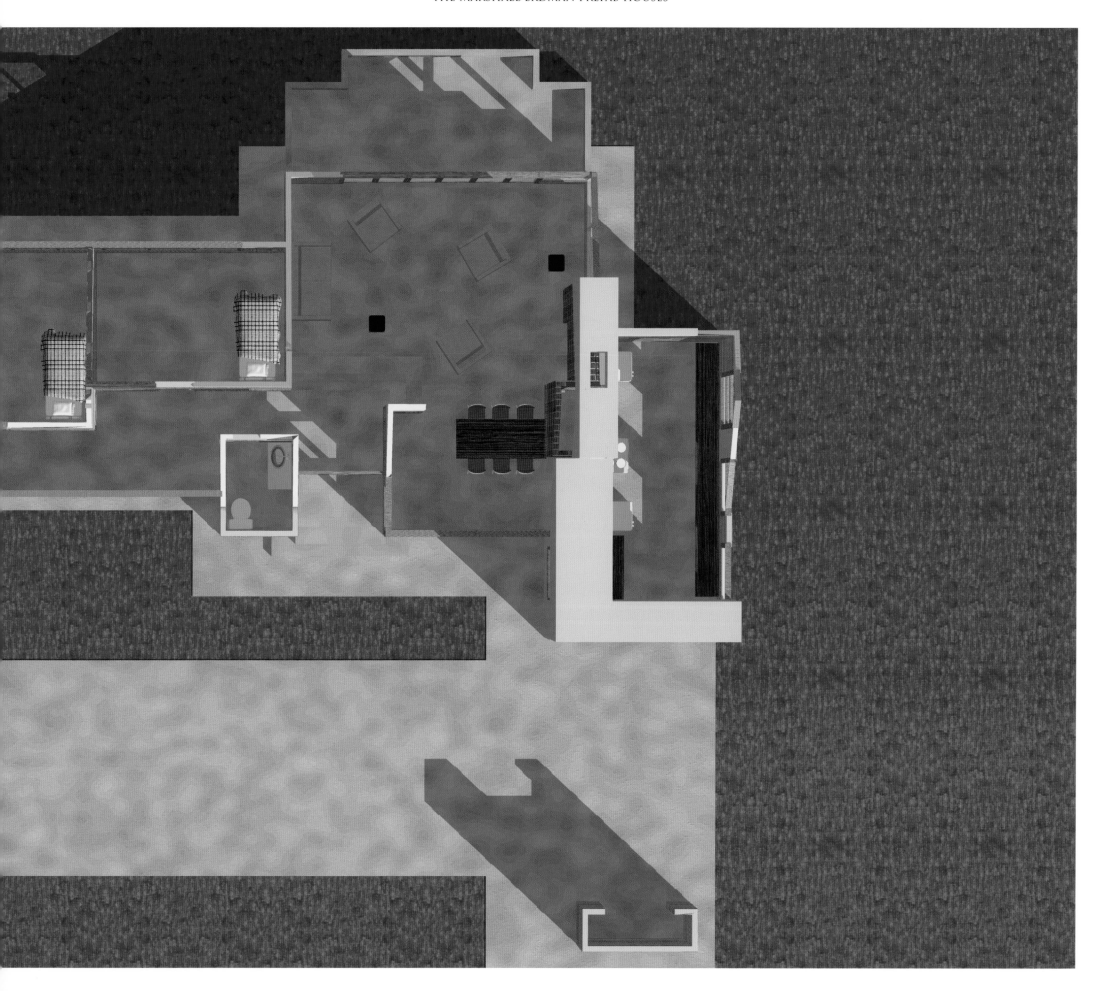

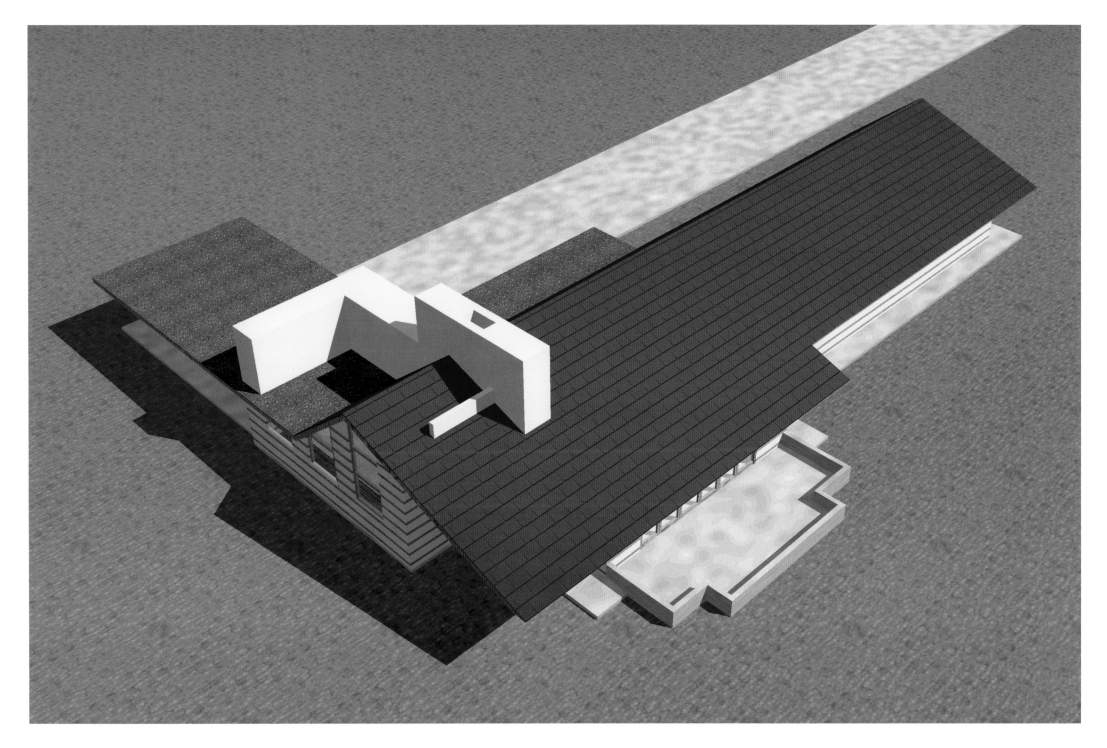

to be spared here, so limestone was used for the masonry and cedar wood for the roof, which is gabled. The exterior paneling is painted, apart from the pale wooden fascia and soffit boards.

The fourth Prefab No. 1 house was the Carl Post Residence in Barrington Hills, Illinois. A builder sold it to Carl Post soon after it was completed in 1957.

The Mollica Residence, in Wisconsin, is the largest of the prefabs. It was built in 1958 for Joseph Mollica, a builder, with four

bedrooms, a workshop, and an exposed basement. A year later, in 1959, came the fifth house, the Cass Residence, built for William and Catherine Cass, this time in New York. It is a four-bedroom version, though with a sixteen-foot-wide master bedroom rather than the standard twelve feet, and has a carport and a basement, at which level there is also a swimming pool. The LaFond Residence in Minnesota, built in 1960, has three bedrooms and a carport plus a basement, where there are four

more bedrooms. In 1961 the Zaferiou Residence was built in New York for Celeste and Socrates Zaferiou. It has four bedrooms, an enclosed basement, a carport, and a workshop. Built from concrete block, it is painted a dark ocher color.

ABOVE: *Frank Lloyd Wright was in his late eighties when he produced three prefabricated houses for the Marshall Erdman Company, but only the first two made it off plan and were actually built.*

RIGHT: *The basic Erdman prefab plan did not allow for a great deal of living space and Wright and Erdman's clients invariably increased the floor plan by extending the principal rooms and adding a fourth bedroom, utility room, and basement.*

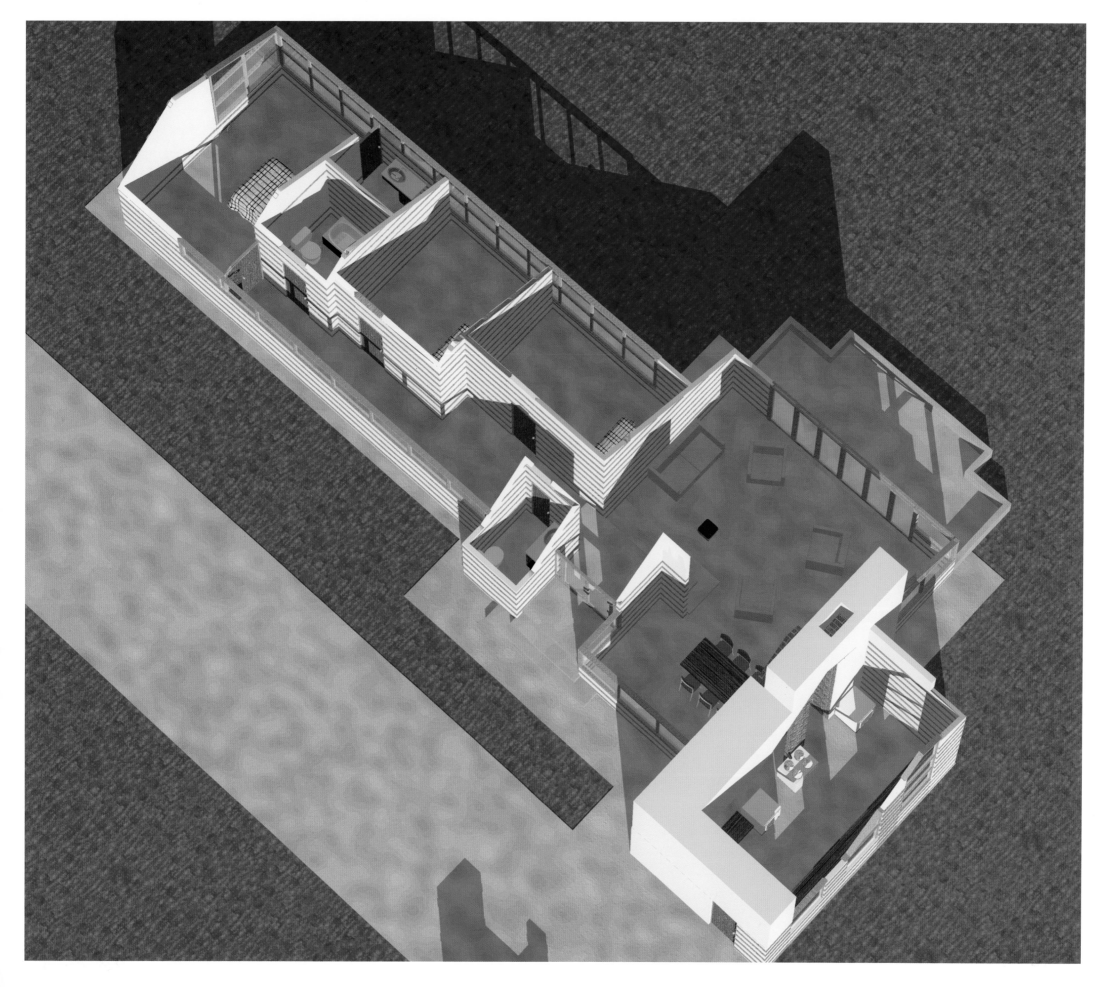

PREFAB NO. 2

Termed the "one-room house," this is a square-plan, flat-roofed building built from the same materials as Prefab No. 1. The two-story living room has windows from floor to ceiling on two sides. On the second level are two bedrooms and a bathroom, with a balcony overlooking the living room. At ground level, the entrance hall separates the kitchen and dining area from the master bedroom, another bathroom and a utility room. A carport and terrace are attached.

The second prefab design to be built, in 1957, was the Rudin Residence in Madison, Wisconsin, for Mary Ellen and Walter Rudin. In the same year the practically identical McBean Residence was built for James B. McBean in Rochester, Minnesota. Unlike the Rudin Residence, though, which is sited on a level plot, this house is set into a hillside and angled to take maximum advantage of the sunlight throughout the day.

In 1958 Wright was still optimistic about the success of the prefabs, and had hopes of finding a least one client in every state. However, the cost-between $30,000 and $50,000-put it out of reach of lower-income families, at whom the concept had been aimed. In 1959 Erdman advertised the designs at a price of $40,000 to $55,000, depending on shipping and local construction costs. At these prices, the houses soon became the choice of well-off people who wanted a Wright-designed house but couldn't afford his custom-built designs, rather than an option for lower-income families.

RIGHT AND FOLLOWING SPREAD: *James B. McBean House, 1957, Rochester, Minnesota, is the second of the three Erdman prefab designs to be built. It sits on a hillside and is angled to catch as much sun as possible throughout the day. It is almost identical to the Walter Rudin Residence. The structure of the house is made of wood with pre-cast concrete blocks which were then painted.*

PAGES 150–151: *Two interior views of the McBean House.*

PREVIOUS PAGE: *Two views of the James B McBean House. This is the Erdman Prefab design #2 that allowed for a second floor. It is built of painted concrete blocks with horizontal batten detailing on plywood panels.*

LEFT AND RIGHT: *Interior views of the James B. McBean House. In all the prefabricated homes the interiors are unconventional (for their period) and provide large open spaces where one area flows into another. Light fittings are sunk into the ceiling so as to provide light without distraction and the stone or brick walls are complimented with the use of hardwood panelling and floors.*

THE HOUSE DESCRIBED

Wright's basic design for the Prefab No. 1 was a single story building of about two thousand square feet with a flat or low-pitched roof. Three bedrooms occupied one end of the rectangle, separated by an open-plan living and dining area from the kitchen, utility room, and bathrooms. A double carport with one end of its roof resting on a detached storage shed completed the design.

The house stood on a slab foundation, which extended four inches beyond the walls to keep water away from the footings and supported joists under a plywood subfloor overlaid with a very hard, red-colored rubber surface scored with "grouting" lines to imitate the appearance of tiles.

Walls were framed with two-inch by four-inch lengths of wood and faced on the inside with sheets of mahogany plywood. On the outside textured Masonite board was lined with horizontal battens. The

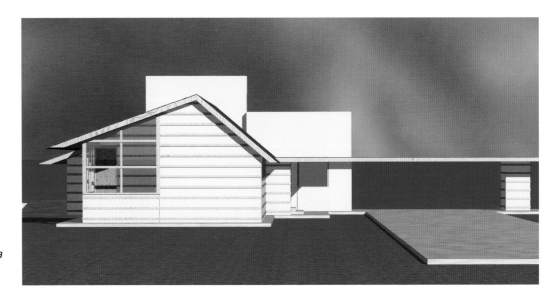

RIGHT, FAR RIGHT AND BELOW: *Interest in the Erdman prefab home was huge after it was featured on a national magazine cover. But buyers proved too few to make the venture a success because the costs proved too high for mass market homes.*

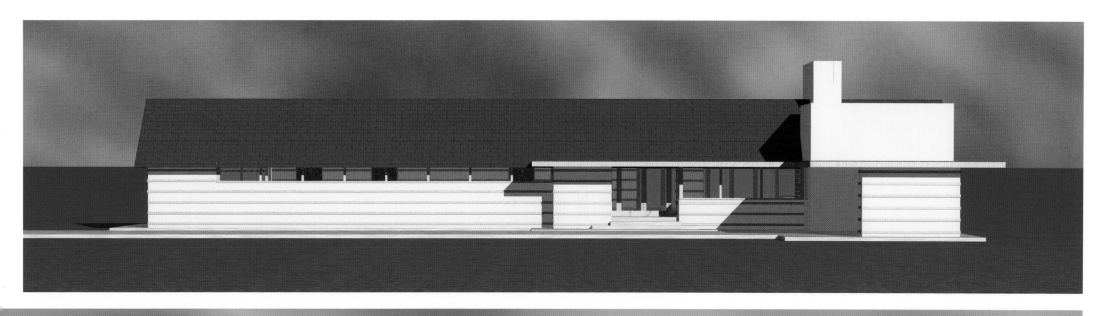

masonry core of the house was centered on a large fireplace. Choices of building material included limestone, brick, or concrete block painted over with linseed oil.

Heating was supplied by a forced-air system that could also accommodate air-conditioning, rather than the gravity heating used in most of Wright's Usonian houses. To save costs, standard ready-made awning windows and doors were used.

Variations on this basic plan included a fourth bedroom (a mirror of the middle bedroom), a garage instead of a carport, a full basement-with or without windows-under the living room, and a workshop. The versions ranged in size from 1,860 to 2,400 square feet. As the plans became more elaborate, so costs increased, pricing the idea out of the market at which it was aimed.

TODAY

The following prefabs were built:

Prefab No. 1
Eugene Van Tamelen Residence (1956)
Jackson Residence (1957)
Duncan Residence (1957)
Frank Iber Residence (1957)
Carl Post Residence (1957)
Mollica Residence (1958)
Cass Residence (1959)
LaFond Residence (1960)
Zaferiou Residence (1961)

Prefab No. 2
Rudin Residence (1957)
Mcbean Residence (1957)

All the prefab houses built by Erdman are now in private ownership.

FAR LEFT AND LEFT: *Living room and utility room in the Frank Iber House.*

NEXT SPREAD: *The Marshal Erdman prefab is a modern icon of simple, elegant design.*

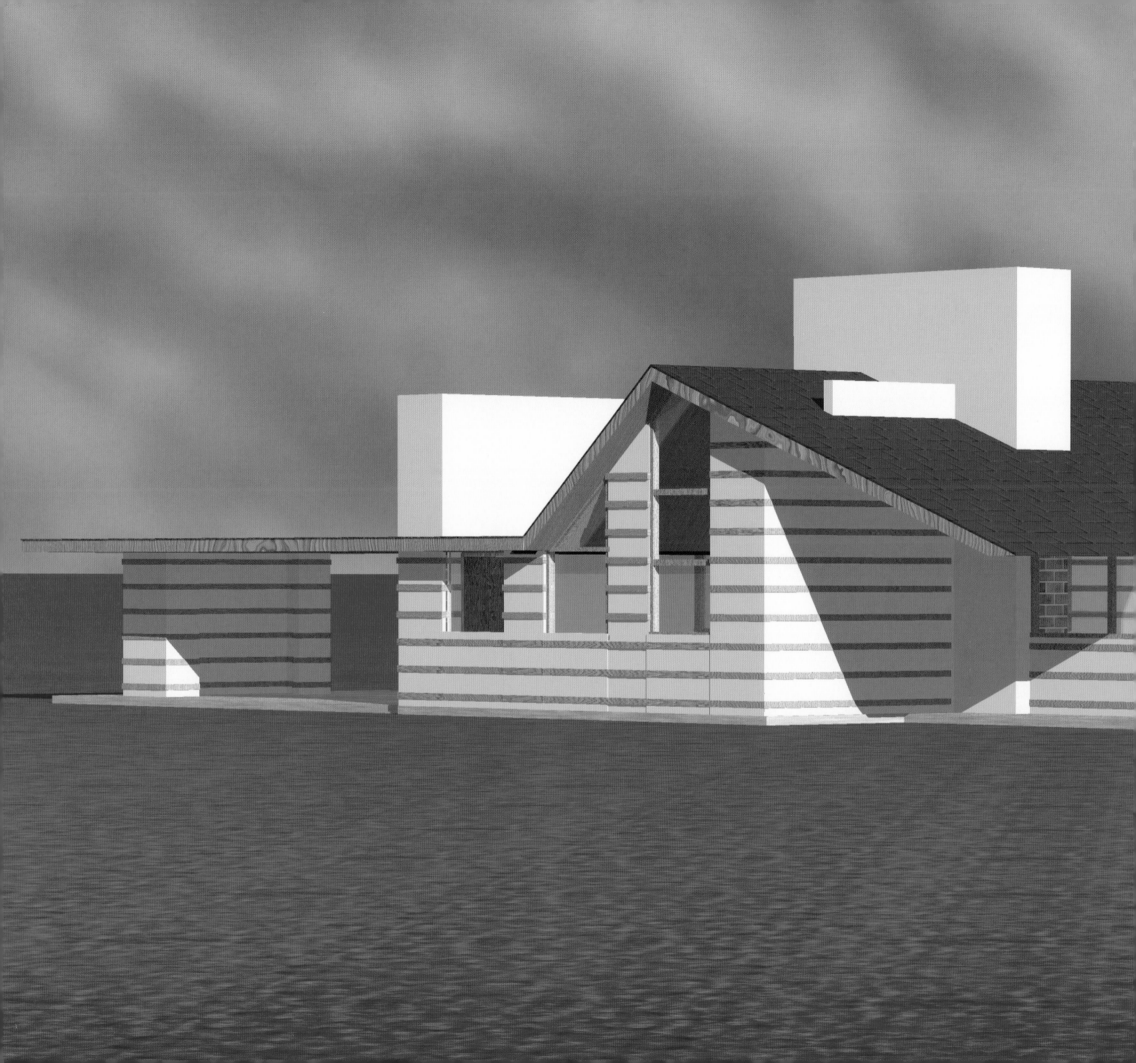

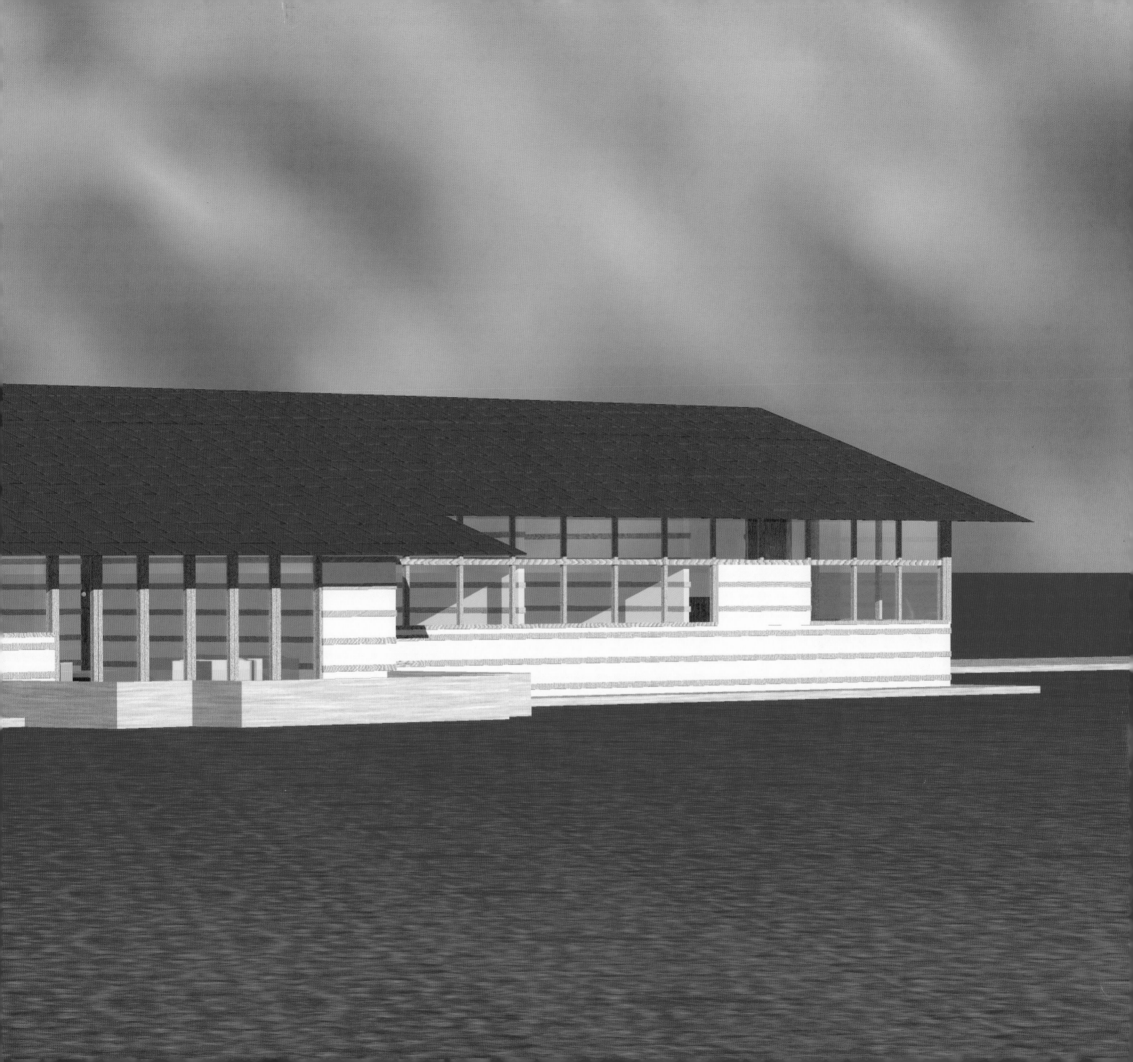

INDEX